AF240900

Children of Gay Couples

Kolia Hiffler-Wittkowsky

CHILDREN OF GAY COUPLES
Stories of Children of Lesbian Couples

Max Milo, Paris, 2023

www.maxmilo.com

ISBN : 978-2-31501-253-4

The *making of*

The why

At the end of 2019, a favorable ruling was handed down for the adoption of my sister and myself by our social mother. This made me realize how important institutional recognition of my family arrangement was to me.

However, I soon realized that we couldn't limit ourselves to state recognition: it had to be complete and unconditional. Yes, unconditional, insofar as our social mother could only be recognized as a mother by providing proof of the reality of her role as a parent. We had to show our credentials, proving to the state that the "us" with which two mothers and two daughters identify forms an acceptable family in the same way as a heteroparental family. This gave me the desire to fight for the full recognition of family configurations similar to mine, namely homoparental families or "rainbow families". It became clear to me that this recognition would never be achieved if we, the people with two mothers born of insemination, a previous hetero union or adoption, were not heard directly.

I designed this book for them, for us and by us... and above all against the editorialists who talk about us without knowing us, gushing about the catastrophe and danger our families would represent for society, or lamenting the fate of poor children raised by two mothers, forever incomplete for not having had the inestimable good fortune to have "a father and a mother". It was time, it was necessary, it was indispensable to make heard what *we* children have to say about our lives and our family experiences. So I decided to call on the pens and voices of the rainbow children I came into contact with or already knew and, more specifically, children who grew up in lesboparental settings, i.e. with two mothers. There's a simple reason for this: I know this family arrangement, because it's mine!

The how

I began by contacting rainbow family associations such as APGL [Association des parents et futurs parents gay et lesbiens[1]] and Enfants d'arc-en-ciel, as well as people I knew more or less closely, to encourage them to take part by giving me their oral or written testimonials. The project immediately aroused great interest. Nathan was the first to answer my questions, then Léa told me she wanted to write her own text; Anne-Lise and her sister Sasha soon joined the project, followed by Maloë, who regularly sent me the elements that eventually made up her testimony; Mathilde, whom I also knew, wrote a longer, more narrative text - all of whom you'll discover in the pages that follow. After that, the number of contributions increased, right up to the end of 2020. As the collection thickened, my knowledge of what children from lesboparental families experience became richer and richer, and I was even more keen to share this wealth of discoveries with as many people as possible.

My role consisted first and foremost in listening to and reading what the people in question had to say and write about their singular

---

1. Association of gay and lesbian parents and parents-to-be.

experience. On a technical level, I coordinated the various testimonies, transcribed the interviews and proofread the texts.

In drawing on these stories, I also wanted to know if the experiences of other rainbow children could be compared to my own. Was it possible, for example, to identify commonalities between the social existence of a non-racialized person and my own, apart from the fact that we have more than one mother? On this point, the testimonies I gathered illustrate the profound heterogeneity of our respective experiences.

The what

The collection comprises two types of texts: on the one hand, interview transcripts, edited by myself and then re-read by the witnesses; on the other, personal texts, written by some children from a lesboparental setting. Some texts are in-between, the reworking of the interview having led to a more narrative form. In all cases, the diversity of aesthetics, both descriptive and analytical, is a choice designed to do justice to the diversity of testimonies.

As for the interviews, I assume their subjectivity. Indeed, my questions were guided by my own experience as a rainbow child, and by a hypothesis according to which our social condition and situation exert a decisive influence on the way we narrate our experiences, as well as on the way we construct our view of the world. This subjectivity nevertheless remained open-ended, as shown by certain witnesses who seriously shook up my presuppositions!

The interviewees were aged between eleven and thirty-one. They were conceived either by MAP, by home-made insemination, or during previous heteroparental relationships. While the family arrangements presented in this collection are extremely diverse, what they have in common is that, to varying degrees no doubt, they escape not only strictly heteroparental structures, but also the decisive presence of cis[2] men in the fundamental family arrangement. I want to show that it is possible to do without the father figure.

Today, there are many of us children living in lesboparent families, and this book proves that we have something to say. I hope that the testimonies gathered in this collection will contribute to the recognition of our experiences, our stories and our subjectivities.

2. Cis (or cisgender) people are those whose gender identity corresponds to the gender assigned to them at birth, unlike transsexual or non-binary people.

Foreword
by Martine Gross, sociologist

The experiences, psyches, well-being, development, gender identity, sexual orientation and other aspects of children raised by two same-sex parents are explored in numerous studies[3] of same-sex families. However, the literature produced by children themselves is extremely marginal. By giving a voice to children raised in lesboparental families, this book both challenges this silence and illustrates the evolution of these families over a generation.

This development was underpinned by transformations in family law and filiation, which gradually led to the recognition of same-sex couples and homoparentality. From the late 1990s to the 2010s, the PACS (1999) and the sharing of parental authority within a lesbian-mother couple (2002) were instituted, followed by marriage for same-sex couples with the possibility of adoption (2013), thus legally protecting children in same-sex families by giving them two legal parents, and finally PMA with filiation established towards both mothers from the child's birth. This last legal provision also includes the right of children to access their donor's identity when they come of age. Some of the young people featured in this book have expressed an interest in this point.

Over the last twenty years or so, same-sex families have seized on all these legal mechanisms. Since the advent of the PACS,

---

3. Vecho, O., & Schneider, B. (2005). "Homoparentalité et développement de l'enfant: bilan de trente ans de publications". *Child Psychiatry, XLVIII* (1), 271-328.

same-sex families have seized on it to build legitimacy[4]. The law of March 4, 2002 enabled a parent to delegate and share parental authority with another person. Several female couples have taken legal action to obtain this right. Apart from this provision, no other possibility existed to give rights to the social parent, the one who did not appear in the family record book[5].

When marriage and adoption were authorized in 2013, many couples of same-sex parents got married. This was not so much a plebiscite for the institution of marriage and the commitment it can represent, but rather for submitting to a necessary condition for the adoption of children by the social parent[6]. Even if lesbian mothers find it distressing to have to adopt their own child in order to have equal rights, intramarital adoption is the only legal means of establishing a child's filiation to both mothers or fathers.

This legal dimension seems very important to parents. Nevertheless, what the children's testimonies gathered here show is that the adoption judgment does not change the affection that existed before. The children already considered their social mother as their mother. In this respect, there was no need to add anything.

*

4. Rault, W. (2005). Construire une légitimité. L'appropriation du pacte civile de solidarité par les familles homoparentales in M. Gross (ed.), *Homoparentalités, état des lieux*, Toulouse, Érès, pp. 319-328.
5. Mécary, C. (2006). What legal protection for children raised by two women or two men? *Dialogue, 173*, 91-102.
6. Stambolis-Ruhstorfer, M., & Descoutures, V. (2020). Licence required: French lesbian parents confront the obligation to marry in order to establish kinship. *International Social Science Journal, 235-236*, 79-97.

In parallel with, and perhaps thanks to, legislative developments, the last 25 years have seen a sociological evolution in same-sex families. I'll just mention the three main aspects.

First of all, the diversity of lesboparental configurations has evolved. To create a lesboparental family, female couples must choose between PMA, co-parenthood or adoption. The distribution of these different options has changed over the last few decades. Female couples are opting more for PMA, and the choice of co-parenthood is declining[7]. Couples who opt for PMA often emphasize the conjugal nature of their parental project, while those who choose co-parenthood weigh up the conjugal nature of the parental project against the desire to give their child a father[8]. When the witnesses in this book talk about their conception, the desire for a child is evoked as emanating naturally from the maternal couple.

Secondly - and this is no doubt a consequence of the previous point - the way in which parents are named changed between the 1990s and the 2010s. In the 1990s and early 2000s, the social mother was called by her first name or a nickname. Few families referred to her as "mom", even when children could say they had two mothers. More and more children raised in lesboparental homes call both women "mom" and say they have two mothers[9]. The testimonials that follow abound in this sense.

---

7. Gross, M., Courduriès, J., & deFederico, A. (2014). Morphology of homoparental families in France in 2012. In A. Fine & J. Courduries (Eds.), *Homosexualité et parenté* (pp. 205-212). Paris : Armand Colin. Gross, M., Courduriès, J., & deFederico, A. (2014). Le recours à l'AMP dans les familles homoparentales : état des lieux. Results of a survey conducted in 2012. *Socio-logos, 9*. Published at http://socio-logos.revues.org/2870.

8. Gross, M. (2009). Les familles homoparentales : entre conformité et innovation. *Informations sociales, 4* (154), 106-114.

9. Gross, M. (2017). Representations of kinship and terms of address in lesboparental families. *Dialogue, 215* (79-94).

Last but not least, and the stories collected here are a reminder of this, even if homophobia has not disappeared, homosexuality seems to be fairly well accepted at school, college and high school. The violence of the debates around marriage for all in 2012-2013 surprised several of the young people interviewed. However, as in Alice Olivier's study[10], young people choose carefully whom they tell that they have two moms. In middle school, they are embarrassed by the pressure to fit in. In high school, on the other hand, they express a certain pride in their slightly different family.

Even if it refutes any scientific vocation, this book provides a deeper understanding of homoparental families and a greater awareness of the diversity of contemporary families in which tenderness, love and affection reign.

---

10. Olivier, A. (2015). "Should I tell them I have two moms?" : careers of (non-)publicizing homoparentality at school in France. *Enfances Familles Génération, 23,* 52-70. Published on http://www.efg.inrs.ca/index.php/EFG/article/view/331.

1.
Anne-Lise, 25 years old

I'd like to be able to tell my story in a different way. For a few years now, I've been telling my story as a rainbow child. I started out in a student association, working with young LGBT people, some of whom are my friends. I had noticed that homosexuals my age still doubted their ability to be good parents. While we had heard too much from homophobes in general and self-proclaimed experts in particular, children themselves were absent from the debate. So it was time for me to tell my story. My testimonies then multiplied: print and radio media, the French National Assembly, conferences, research...

I was born on a Tuesday, in April 1995, at snack time. My mothers had met eight years earlier, at the home of mutual friends. At the time, there was a legal vacuum in France regarding the precise conditions of access to Medically Assisted Procreation (MAP). The 1994 bioethics law reserved it for heterosexual couples. My moms appealed to the French Medical Association, which, by one vote, refused them access to PMA in France. Although a number of associations for same-sex families already existed, they were little-known and mainly focused on the Paris region. It was by chance, during a report in a specialized infertility department at the Erasmus hospital in Belgium, that they discovered a solution for their parental project. I was conceived in Brussels, by artificial insemination with a third-party donor.

My moms were very well received, but they told me that they felt the delays imposed by the procedure, and the feeling that they were being tested to see if they would be good parents, were a source of violence. Of course, this PMA process abroad represented a significant financial and psychological cost. How can you not feel hurt when you are a citizen of one country and have to go to another to build your family? This struggle to become mothers, despite obstacles and prejudice, this courage not to doubt yourself when society sends you back a negative image of yourself, this will and this love, these are common fuels to all children conceived by MAP. We are all sure that we were wanted, and so we enter life with an irreplaceable asset.

People often ask me when I knew where I came from. I've always known! My mothers never hid anything from me. They explained my conception to me, adding more and more complex information as I grew up. Encountering other children, at the nanny's and then at school, naturally led me to reflect on the difference between my family and others. I say "the others", because the classic mom-dad model was no longer in the majority. Single-parent and blended families predominated.

As long as I was little, life was pretty easy. The other kids hadn't yet integrated homophobic ideas. My friends envied me for having "two moms". On Father's Day, I'd make a present at school for my second mom, my "social mom". I invited my girlfriends over. I didn't hide. My mothers were cautious about meeting with the management of each of the schools my sister and I attended, to discuss their homoparenting and make sure it wasn't a problem. They never had a problem. My second mother, and I'll come back to this, had no legal relationship with us, but she was always able to sign the parental authorization documents for the school. In other words, the state that excludes us includes us; it ignores us and takes us into account.

*

Things got complicated when I grew up. I went to a big Catholic school in the city, and I didn't dare talk about my family. Nothing was adapted, my parents were invisible. At the start of each school year, I had to fill out a dozen administrative documents in which my teachers asked me: "Father's first and last name, father's profession." What if you don't have a father? Where do I put my two moms on your form? When they asked me what my father did, I'd answer: carpenter!

Today, I'm ashamed of having been ashamed. It was hard for me to accept that I was different, at an age when you absolutely want to be like your peers. I only spoke about my moms to a few friends I trusted. With them, everything went well. On the other hand, in some catechism classes, I was shocked to hear that love is between a man and a woman. It also offended some of my classmates. Some parents contacted the school's principal education advisor to stop this kind of talk being made in class. I was very touched by this mobilization, and I discovered the importance of having allies.

The debate on marriage for all, in 2012 and 2013, changed everything. My little world, relatively protected from hatred until then, was turned upside down by the homophobic comments of opponents, relayed by the media. To believe them, my parents were pedophiles or zoophiles unworthy of marriage. Hundreds of thousands of people marched in the streets to oppose my family's rights. Their speeches were heard on radio and television. They were on posters and in debates everywhere! The subject was suffocating me.

1. Anne-Lise, 25 years old

All the more so as it became an integral part of our discussions with friends. I felt obliged to *come out.* I couldn't talk about it as if I didn't know. People I'd been seeing for seven years distanced themselves from me. One of them told me that homosexuality was hereditary. So if we legalized same-sex families, one day everyone would be homosexual. I argued: my grandparents aren't homosexuals; however, they had homosexual children... who had a heterosexual daughter, me! Still, the accumulation of prejudices ended up being painful.

Nevertheless, this ordeal had one quality: it politicized me. I wanted to get involved, to be a player in this debate. The postponement and then cancellation of the vote on PMA for all reinforced this desire. I stopped hiding. When the subject of parents came up in conversation, I talked about my moms. My studies led me to be surrounded by peers who were often closer to my political opinions and mostly open-minded on the subject of homoparentality. I ended up protecting myself by excluding people with homophobic tendencies from my social circle. However, I always wait until I know someone well before telling them about my parents. I don't want my identity to be reduced to this singularity, and for my person to be interpreted in the light of my parents' homosexuality.

*

Then something new happened. I discovered that not only could the people I confided in tolerate me, but they could also be very, very happy to meet me! For the first time, I understood that my family's difference was also an asset.

And yet, as I was saying, I'd like to be able to testify in a different way. Because, for me, testifying is as much a liberation as a new

prison. You have to give a good account of yourself and your family, and show that you've "made it". This requirement is accentuated at a time when we are debating the extension of PMA to women's couples. Since we're discussing the desirability of allowing lesbians to have children, we have to say that everything's going well for us, don't we? The slightest sign of weakness, misfortune or failure, although common to all families, can be interpreted as resulting from my parents' homosexuality. So I have to prove, through every testimony, that I'm "normal". Always with the same three arguments:
- I studied,
- I'm not crazy, and the icing on the cake,
- I'm not homosexual.
Isn't it incredibly homophobic to see a problem in the fact that homosexuals might have homosexual children themselves? My mothers' homosexuality has, I think, made me more open-minded about gender and sexuality. Who's ever watched *Priscilla, madwoman of the desert* with their family? I love this glittery, colorful world. I love the rainbow flag, pride marches, *drag queens* and the Sisters of Perpetual Indulgence. I know perfectly well what happened during the AIDS epidemic, the homophobic insults, all the discrimination that homosexuals can suffer. I feel free to love whoever I want, whatever their gender identity, and to express my femininity as I wish. My sister Sasha and I have heated debates at home because my mothers are not from the same generation as us. But the LGBT community has evolved so much... So my mothers are bringing themselves up to date through us. No choice!

I've had a feminist upbringing, in the sense that my parents have never told me I can't do or have something because I'm a girl, and because they howl at the TV when a misogynist speaks. They're very

1. Anne-Lise, 25 years old

adamant about women's free disposal of their bodies. However, I quickly realized that they too, because they are the product of our society and not extraterrestrials, have integrated gender norms and reproduce them.

My mother, the one who bore us, is more feminine and takes care of the tasks usually associated with women. My second mother, more masculine, takes care of the other tasks. In short, I was being a smart-aleck about *Priscilla, madwoman of the desert earlier,* but in reality, we grew up in a family that perfectly inculcated society's norms in us!

The proof: my parents' homosexuality didn't make me think about my gender identity. I discovered transidentity late in life, during my studies. Meeting my transgender classmates really shook me up. I feel like a woman, and I don't think it's important to be a woman until it's used to restrict me. I'm attracted to all bodies, but so far I've only been in love with boys.

When people ask me:

- What about your father?

I answer that I don't have a father, not in the sense of a man who raises me as his daughter. I know that male gametes are needed to make a child. In Belgium, donors are anonymous. I know how tall mine is, what color his eyes and hair are, that's all. I also know that he donated when PMA was still relatively unknown to the general public. I deduce that he was probably a medical student aware that his donation could benefit a couple of women. He must have been ahead of his time, altruistic and open-minded. He made a magnificent and courageous donation, for a reason of his own, and if genes are to have any meaning at all, I'm proud to be the product of such a gesture.

*

For me, genetic history is irrelevant.

I don't ask myself which part of my body comes from my sire, and which from my mother. In France at the moment, there's a lot of debate about "access to origins", because children conceived by PMA in our country within heterosexual couples have suffered from the long-standing secrecy surrounding their conception. It's difficult to cultivate the same secrecy in female couples, but I think it's a good idea to give children the possibility of exchanging information with their parent if they feel the need to do so.

So, among the recurring questions, there are also :

- And you, would you have liked to talk with your sire?

After changing my mind fifty times, I'd say yes. Yes, I'd be curious to know the context in which he made this donation, his motivations. However, I would be afraid, I think, because this man is not my father. There are no established social codes to govern the relationship you can have with a donor. My sister and I don't have the same donor, but we have the same parents. I don't want to think of her as my half-sister!

*

My all-female nuclear family hasn't stopped me from having male figures around me. The closest is my godfather. I also have a grandfather, cousins and the fathers of my childhood friends. In short, even if I still can't knot a tie, I live in a mixed world that my parents' homosexuality never concealed. The real problem is that, until 2013, I had no way of establishing a legal parent-child relationship with my social mother. As PMA is forbidden in France

1. Anne-Lise, 25 years old

for female couples, there was no question of providing a way for them to be linked to their children. The woman who gives birth is a mother under French law. She is not asked how she conceived her child. For the second woman, it's anguish. It's impossible to authorize an operation on her child, or to assert custody rights in the event of separation.

So my mothers have multiplied alternative safety nets. For example, my second mother is my godmother in the eyes of... the Church! That's right. At the age of two, I was baptized by a priest who was perfectly aware of the situation. My godmother was my social mother.

When the law on marriage for all was passed in May 2013, I was already 18. But when my grandmother died in 2016, I felt an urgent need to formalize our family, to protect us from the vagaries of life. Because, now, I'm the one who can't authorize an operation for my social mother, should she need it one day and my other mother be absent. That's why my mothers got married in 2017, and why we then applied to the judge for adoption. Simple adoption, because my sister and I are of age; and adoption tout court because it's the only way.

Need I explain how absurd it seemed to me to have my mother adopt me, just as it seemed absurd to my mother to adopt her own child? Anyway, I was happy to know that I was finally going to have a family record book with the four of us, and that my social mother would be recognized for her true worth.

The fact remains that putting together the application was epic. The simple adoption application form was not adapted to our situation. Once again, we didn't fit into any of the boxes! We had to provide the judge with proof that my mother had raised my sister and me properly, family photographs and testimonials from our friends and teachers. The application was processed quickly; we were not summoned to appear before the judge; and we were thrilled to receive the registered letter announcing the favorable decision. Even our postmistress was moved!

What about today? I work in a team that fights homophobia at state level, and in which I can freely talk about my family. I'm delighted to have the chance to get involved in this subject, which touches me deeply, but it's very demanding to deal professionally with such personal issues. To launch the examination of the bill on opening PMA to all women, Agnès Buzyn - then Minister of Health - recognized the existence and legitimacy of our families. It sent shivers down my spine.

I think a lot about the children conceived today by PMA in lesbian couples, about the lightning evolution of French society on this subject in twenty-five years. I'm reassured for them. They won't grow up thinking they're alone in this situation. They'll find albums representing their family. They'll face more appropriate forms. Their legal security will be established. On the other hand, sexism and homophobia have not disappeared, and I hope they will have the resources to confront them. It's for them that I testify here. For them and for their parents.

2.
Interview with Audrey, 26

Can you briefly introduce yourself?

My name is Audrey, I'm twenty-six, I live in Montpellier and work in the audiovisual industry.

Can you tell us about the changes that have taken place in your family?

My mother was married to my father, then got involved with a woman after they separated. My mother has never loved a man other than my father in her whole life, and she has never loved a woman other than the one she is with now, even though she has had other stories.

When did your parents separate?

I must have been eight or nine. I remember the first time my mother introduced me to her new girlfriend. Just because she wasn't my dad, I had a huge rejection towards her. For a week, I refused to talk to her. It was my mother who reminded me of this episode, years later. After a few months, my mother and her girlfriend separated for the first time. However, this woman continued to check up on me and to be there for me. This made me realize that I loved her very much, not because she was my mother's girlfriend, but because I loved who she was. When she and my mother got back together, I really felt like I was back with my family. She too had had children of her own, two daughters, after a heterosexual relationship, just like my mother. We ended up being one big family: my brother, his two daughters who are now my sisters, and my moms, as I've called them ever since.

Do you call your second mother "Mom"?

Never. When I speak of them in the plural, I say "my moms"; when I speak of them individually, I say "Mom" and "Alex". I call her "Alexandria". I'm the only one [Audrey is a non-binary person who uses the masculine and feminine indiscriminately to talk about herself] to call her that.

Has there been a change in the distribution of roles at home? Have you noticed a different way of dealing with authority?

At home, it's always been pretty clear: my mother is my authority figure, Alex is my sisters'. For me, Alex has been more of a calming figure, offering advice and a kind look, sometimes in my relationship with my mother too. The roles at home are shared between the two of them. They do the housework and the shopping together. They cook according to their desires and availability. Even when they're feeling lazy, they're in it together!

What is your mothers' relationship with politics? Do you know if they vote? What can you say about their relationship to religion and your own?

My mothers vote. I know Alex sees politics as something very intimate, so I'll respect that here and say no more. They are both believers and churchgoers to some extent. I'm a believer too, I was very religious when I was younger. Now it's complicated. Religion shouldn't be an opposition to the love that people have for each other or for another person, regardless of the gender of the people involved. I'm frustrated by the current situation, but I can see the progress, particularly in the Pope's speech, in talking about France's number one religion. I have a feeling that, in a few decades' time, we'll be able to have more recognition within different religions. I'd like to make it clear that my conception of religion is specific. I'm in a relationship with a God and with the things of the universe that I've created for myself over the years. I detect three elements: a Christian influence, a pinch of Wiccan and a good deal of free will.

How did your schooling go? Did you talk to your classmates about your situation?

At school, it didn't go down well, in the sense that it was hidden, it was taboo. Only extremely close friends knew about it. I went to high school at the time of marriage for all, when the people I saw as friends thought it was just a discussion, saying that the children of homosexuals would never be happy. My whole school career was extremely complicated, because I started using the taboo as a weapon to say to people: "Shut up! I'm happy and fuck you! It was like my moms *coming out to me*, even though I'm just their daughter... I became the standard-bearer for a cause, when all I cared about was living my life and not having my family insulted just because they weren't "right".

And at university?

Then I started hanging out more in *queer* circles. In that context, my situation seemed much more normal! When I said "my moms", nobody was shocked, and that was a relief.

Have you met any other rainbow children?

My mother knew a lot of lesbians who'd had heterosexual relationships. So, throughout my teenage years, the picture I had of homoparental families was of parents who had been in straight unions before. Then, when I grew up, when I went to university and got really interested in these issues, I met people who had transitioned, who had been in straight couples and formed gay couples... I met a range of parents and families, and that did me a lot of good, because, in the end, it trivialized things.

What was the meaning of this coming out? *Was it a* coming out *for your mothers, or was it you who, through them, experienced this coming out of the closet?*

I came to terms with my bisexuality before I came to terms with the fact that my mother was a lesbian. But I realized that she herself had a lot of trouble accepting it. I think she was afraid people would treat me badly because she was with a woman. Strangely enough, I experienced *coming out* as a political tool as the daughter of a lesbian, not as a bi person.

Is the fact that you've been able to come to terms with your bisexuality due to growing up in an open environment?

Yes, but not on my mother's side, because when I tried to broach the subject with her, she said, "You're too young" and "I wish you weren't." We talked about it again years later, and she said things like: "I've suffered so much, I don't want you to go through what I've been through. That's why I don't want you to be bi." I first *came out to* her when I was thirteen, but I had to come out again more recently, for her to take me seriously. It was an open and caring environment, especially coming from my uncle. He took me seriously right away.

Is your uncle involved?

He's been openly *queer* for some years now. When I was a teenager, he labeled himself homosexual.

Are there other queer *or LGBTQIA+ people in your family?*

No, they didn't. When I *came out for the* third time as a non-binary person, they all looked at me with wide eyes… except my uncle. It was he who, seeing how passionate I was about the issue, asked me the question and helped me become aware of who I am.

What political tools does this situation provide you with?

The situation doesn't provide me with political tools, it plunges me *de facto* into political issues. The problem is that when you have a minority identity, you're always a political tool. When there were all those debates about marriage, adoption and PMA, it was as if the children of homosexuals didn't yet exist, as if there weren't any. Speaking out at the time felt almost like an obligation. If you keep quiet, if you don't take sides at that moment, you're depriving all the other people who would like to have that kind of happiness. I have the impression that my situation implies a political obligation to take a stand.

Do you think every rainbow child has a duty to testify?

The fact that we don't fit in with the norms (with lots of quotation marks) is already a battle in itself that's imposed on us. Whether we talk about it, hide it or use it as a weapon to piss others off, everyone does what they can at the time. It can evolve over the course of our lives: there are times when we doubt ourselves and don't feel legitimate, others when we're ready to kick some ass… So, to the question: "Should we testify?", the answer is: "Yes, if we have the strength to do so, we should, because it also helps people who don't."

Have you ever wanted to have children?

Yes, I was with someone for many years and fell in love with her deeply. From the moment we met, I was convinced that she was the one for me, that we were going to get married and have children together. Sometimes life doesn't care about our plans, it has to be said. Today, I don't know if I'll ever love her that much again, or if I'll ever build a relationship on that model (and if I do, sorry partner from the future, I didn't even know you existed when I said that!). On the other hand, in a few years, I'm thinking of adopting a child. I can't see myself creating a life in the world around us anymore, but taking care of a breath that's already there and alone, that would suit me.

Are you involved in any associations, parties or other political structures that would lead these struggles on a collective scale?

When I was in Paris, I approached associations. The problem was that it didn't suit me.

Why?

In associations, there are often personal stories between people, headaches and power plays. I didn't want to reproduce on a small scale what I criticize in the surrounding world. As a result, my way of fighting was more about communication, benevolence and exchanging with people... Paradoxically, sometimes I went to the general assemblies of associations I wasn't a member of. When I was in Paris, I used to go to the night Pride, which I felt was much more important than the day Pride: I felt that the night Pride brought a much more political and anti-establishment perspective. I'm more at ease when I'm involved in these little loops of life than in a big organization.

What's your take on the struggles of sexual and gender minorities in our society?

I'm not apolitical, but I'm disgusted by all the movements... I don't believe in the current Republic. I have more affinity with anarchism and self-management. Intersectional feminism also stimulates me. The moment you start taking an interest in a minority, you fight for all equalities, I find that logical. So we have to stand together for equality in general, not just for equality of origin or gender or sexuality... There can be no individual equity without collective equity. That's also why the currents I'm generally involved with insist on the importance of popular education.

What do you mean by that?

Not just an education for political emancipation, but also an education to understand and accept the people around us. I think that people today can understand "rainbow children". On the other hand, I have the impression that, in France, the fight we're furthest behind in is on gender issues, even if there's also a long way to go on the rest; and I believe that the necessary deconstruction implied by this concept is compatible with libertarian and anarchist ideas.

In your opinion, are there any rights left to be wrested, or is it not on the ground of rights that we have to fight?

We don't have a choice! On the subject of rights, let me give you a concrete answer: I'm not interested in getting married. However, some people dream of it all their lives, and I have no desire to take that away from them. So we have to be proactive and vigilant. In my opinion, there's a risk of losing marriage for all at any moment, but there are obviously a lot of battles to be fought in parallel. To change this system, we've got to get going, guys!

3.
Sasha, 22 years old

When I say my parents are gay, most of the time the first question I'm asked is about my birth. It varies from person to person, but I'm often offered an explanation that seems the most plausible: "Did your mother leave your father and marry a woman?" or "Were you adopted?" or even, "Did your father die?". Eventually, the answer became automatic:

- No, I just don't have a father, my moms went to Belgium to have PMA for my sister Anne-Lise and for me.

So the conversation usually turns to what PMA is, which mother carried me, why in Belgium... I'm usually a bit surprised when I explain that PMA is forbidden in France for female couples: while these people knew nothing about homoparentality ten minutes earlier, the idea that two people who love each other could be forbidden from simply having children seems as absurd to them as it does to me.

I've been hearing these questions since I was a little girl. As early as elementary school, if the conversation turned to my parents, it seemed natural to tell the others that my parents are two women. At least to avoid confusion, to avoid having to skirt around the subject or avoid pronouns at all costs. At that age, telling people was more a matter of pragmatism than anything else. I was a talker, I always had lots to say on lots of subjects, and my moms were simply part of my life. I used to talk about them as part of my identity, in the same way that, today, loving sushi and riding a bike are part of who I am. I've known people for years without them knowing, simply because we never talked about our parents. On the contrary, after talking to someone for ten minutes, I sometimes mention it during the conversation.

During adolescence, as I was learning to assert myself through my similarities and differences, my family's exceptional status became a way of distinguishing me from the rest of my peers. Reactions were mixed, from the most inappropriate (like: "Oh, *cool!* I love lesbian porn!") to the most appropriate, i.e. welcoming the information as a simple fact. That was my norm, of course, but at the time I wasn't aware that it wasn't for the vast majority of people around me. For me, homophobia was a distant concept, with which I had very little contact. What I saw up until then was mainly my family's fear of homophobia: my moms never held hands in public, my sister rarely told her friends… In my everyday life, homophobia seemed disparate, almost minimal and, above all, hidden.

So much so that, in 2013, when the issue of "marriage for all" began to be seriously addressed by the government, the wave of hatred it generated was particularly violent and on a scale I would never have imagined. I used to dream that the first wedding I'd attend would be my moms', and that dream turned into months of gritting my teeth in the face of public homophobia. Every week, the news showed thousands of people marching in the streets, crying out for the institution of a marriage they'd always had the privilege of, and for the protection of children they knew nothing about. I kept asking myself: how can they spew their prejudices and reject my family without knowing us? I was outraged that their comments were tolerated.

Having homosexual parents was no longer a simple fact of life: it was a reason for militancy. When "marriage for all" was finally passed, I saw it as a victory *for* my parents and *against* homophobes; however, as the law stopped just before PMA, my sister Anne-Lise and I knew we'd have to face a similar battle a few years later.

In the meantime, I was able to live my little girl's dream and, above all, I was finally able to see my social mother recognized as such, after she had wanted me, raised me and loved me as her child. Today, the fact that I was able to live at a time when "marriage for all" was not legal seems almost insane. And yet, it's not as if I didn't experience certain forms of invisibilization of my family by society. For example, the forms I had to fill in for school, on which I would cross out the mention of "father" in the information about my parents. Similarly, my social mother's status has always needed to be clarified because it's outside the norm.

*

In a way, having two moms opened up my mind, because I knew *it* existed, that *it* worked and therefore that *it* could be experienced by lots of people around me just as I was experiencing it myself. It was much more real in my mind than in that of many of my peers. But beyond that, I don't think I was particularly well-informed. My moms had always wanted to live their lives like everyone else, while my sister and I gradually took up more and more militant positions. It was on the Internet, when I was in high school, that I discovered that being LGBT+ wasn't just limited to *gay* and lesbian couples, that there were so many more sexualities and gender identities. I understood that being LGBT+ was both a story of individual identity and a story of a community united across similarities and differences.

Thanks to this process, I was able to put words to things I felt, such as the attraction to both boys and girls that gripped me during

3. Sasha, 22 years old

my teenage years. I might as well say that my *coming out wasn't* really that difficult after that: my friends had no problem with homosexuality, and my family even less so. When I went off to Paris for higher education, I met like-minded LGBT+ people who saw my gay moms as a hope for their own future. So we took great pleasure in tearing down the posters of La Manif Pour Tous and laughing at the homophobes.

In the same vein, I began to explore questions around my gender, its expression, what it meant to me to be a woman. Our mothers brought us up more as children than as little girls, although this didn't mean that certain typically feminine "qualities" weren't instilled in us. I had to behave and dress in a way that was relatively associated with the "girl" stereotype, but I wasn't often chastised when I adopted attitudes that were considered more masculine. However, I did observe a relatively heteronormative version of the couple in my parents' behavior. So much so that the idea of what it was to be a woman remained anchored in me as embodied by my biological mother, while my social mother had taken on a more typically masculine role.

This distribution is far from insignificant. Indeed, society's preoccupation with the family generally concerns the absence of a man. As if the only man likely to influence a child's life were his father! I've always known men around me: a godfather, neighbors, my parents' friends, my own friends... What's more, the idea that at least one man and one woman are absolutely necessary to bring up a child properly strikes me as reductive. It denies all nuance, pits femininity against masculinity, and tries to hide each person's specific personality traits behind fragile clichés.

Among the male figures, both present and absent, is my donor. I appreciate his gesture because he thought of a couple who wanted children but couldn't have any, and because he had, without realizing it, a major role in the long obstacle course my moms led. Apart from that, he's as much my father as any stranger I meet on the street. Ever since I was a little girl, my idea of family has gone beyond the question of blood. My social mother has played as formative a role in my life as my biological mother. My sister, who didn't have the same donor as me and is therefore technically my "half-sister", has never been less than my sister in my eyes; and our relationship is much closer than some people I've known with their own siblings.

Going beyond my own family, I've often come across evidence that biology as the only link isn't enough: you need love and a willingness to do what's right for your child. At least, that's a good start! I've seen friends whose heterosexual parents were absent or abusive; I've known parents who will probably never know their child's homosexuality because the child knew full well that they would reject him or her; and I've seen so-called "traditional" heterosexual families; loving, friends whose parents were divorced, whose siblings came from a different marriage, whose stepfather or stepmother was very present. I've been with single-parent families. Homoparenting isn't the only way to question the single family model! The idea that parenthood is essentially biological seriously needs to be put into perspective...

At the end of the day, gay or straight, we're all the same. I'm convinced that if I'd met more homoparental families, I'd have come across just as many different family forms as in heterosexual households. Logical: homosexuality is really only a small part of us.

*

3. Sasha, 22 years old

In the parents' lottery, I feel I've been lucky. In a way, PMA and the obstacles that go with it are undeniable proof that we were wanted children. However, far be it from me to proclaim that my moms are perfect, or that they've always been the best parents in the world. That's where the difficulty of testifying comes in. You want to present yourself in the best possible light and shout:

- Look, I'm normal, I'm perfectly balanced and my moms don't have any faults!

We know - or *at least* fear - that anything less than excellence can be used against us. The slightest flaw becomes suspect. The slightest hint of something out of the ordinary would justify homosexual couples not having as much right to PMA as heterosexuals. Now, yes, my moms have flaws, but not because they're homosexual. Just because they're human. And me, can I admit that I'm not always well, can I even say that I'm bisexual without people shaking their heads and saying, "Of course, with two moms..."?

I admit that, by testifying, I censor myself in order to show society that I conform to its criteria for self-fulfilment. I speak less for myself than for others, with the more or less assumed idea of reassurance. Yes, a two-woman couple can raise their children well. They can be gay or straight. They can have a successful life, just like any other child. And, no, just like "marriage for all", granting rights to homosexual couples is not dangerous and takes nothing away from anyone.

At the end of my story, I'd like to correct my message. Sometimes I have to overcome trials and face difficulties, but very few of them have anything to do with my mothers' sexuality. When this is the case, the problem doesn't come from my parents or me: it's always caused by the way my family is viewed. Ultimately, I'm delighted if I can have a positive impact on a few people's vision by showing them that my family is just as legitimate as theirs. That's why, when I testify orally, awkward and repetitive questions no longer annoy me. The truth is, they're just as important as what I say. A question, whatever it may be, remains an opening and a door to better understanding.

Without communication, without dialogue, without the exploration of otherness, we go straight to the wall. We lock ourselves into our own ideas, prejudices and beliefs, and ignorance risks mutating into hatred. Telling my story contributes to the normalization of the same-sex family. This is all the more important as everyone has a lesbian aunt, cousin or neighbor; and I hope that, in a few years' time, that aunt, cousin or neighbor will have children for whom answering their classmates' questions about their mothers and PMA will have become as automatic as it has become for me.

4.
Interview with Elsa, 20

Can you tell me how you were conceived?

My little sister and I were conceived in Belgium by donor insemination. We both had the same donor, but not the same biological mother. Both our mothers had the idea of having children in the second half of the 1990s. It wasn't possible for them, as a couple of homosexual women, to carry out an ADI [Artificial Insemination with Donor] in France. Hence Belgium. After seven attempts, my mom became pregnant with me. Two years later, it was my other mom's turn to get pregnant with my little sister.

Are your mothers still together?

Yes, they got married in 2013 as soon as the law on marriage for all was passed. They took turns adopting us. My sister and I both grew up with our two moms from the start.

Do you know anything about the donor?

As this is an anonymous donation, we have very little information about him. We know that he was in favor of helping a couple of women have children. We know that he himself already had one or more children, and we also know his skin color. That's all we know.

Do you ever speculate about this person?

I never think about her because she's not part of my daily life. I know nothing about him. If I met him, it would be pure curiosity, to find out what he looks like physically.

With no father and two mothers, how was your family perceived at school?

My moms were quite close to my teachers and sometimes their friends, especially in elementary school, so everyone knew.

You mean it was easy?

At first, yes. I had a bit of trouble with having to cross out the word "father" and replace it with "mother". Apart from that, there weren't really any problems for me or my sister. We were lucky enough to grow up in an open and tolerant environment. Whether it was neighborhood life or elementary school, people were *cool.*

What next?

From middle school onwards, I became aware of the importance of other people's opinions, and I was afraid that the many Muslim students around me would take offense. Which goes to show that *prejudices aren't* just for homophobes! In short, for fear of ridicule and insults, I would only talk about my family situation to my close friends. In high school, things got better. Most people were openly tolerant. I was better able to accept the peculiarity of my family model... and even to promote this originality!

Is the openness you describe linked to a specific social milieu?

We grew up in a very non-religious neighborhood. The majority of families were economically in the upper-middle class. I think this helped open up most of these people.

What professions do your mothers practise?

They don't have the same field of action at all! My biological mother is a researcher. My other mother works in an association linked to the principles of non-conventional education.

You're in your second year of a bachelor's degree in Korean...

Yes, and it's great because people who are interested in Korea and Korean music groups are often more open about homosexuality. But, well, in general, at university, there are also a lot of environmentalist, feminist and Marxist groups who are in favor of rights for all. So it's a pretty comfortable place for me!

Have you ever felt discriminated against or oppressed in any way?

I have a memory from middle school that comes back to me a lot. I had to make fun of a boy in my class, and he threatened to tell another boy in the class about my family situation. I begged him not to. In the end, this young North African spoke to his neighbor in Arabic, and I could see them laughing at me because I had two mothers. I felt really bad that day. We were all young and stupid. I forgive them.

Do you remember the debates on "marriage for all"?

We used to talk about it a lot at home, because it was all over the news for quite a while, all those debates, all those demonstrations for all, well, rather "against all"... I remember my sister

4. Interview with Elsa, 20

and I were shocked by the words of the extremist Catholics who said: "Afterwards, I'll marry my goat", or something like that. And I remember how happy I was because my moms would finally be able to get married, and we'd finally be able to be adopted by our non-biological mother.

Was the fact that you could be adopted important to you?

Before marriage and adoption, my biological mother always told me that, if anything happened to her, my aunt (her little sister) would have more rights over me than my other mother, even though I only see my aunt once a year and, for thirteen years, I've lived with both my mothers, whom I call "Mum". For us, it was important to know that if something happened to one of our mothers, the other would have the same rights as the missing one. Before marriage and adoption, my non-biological mother had no rights over me, whether in terms of school, institutions or even family names. I couldn't officially have my social mother's surname. In my family record book, there was only my biological mother and me; there was no mention of my other mother or my little sister. Symbolically, marriage and adoption were very important, for my sister and for me. Today, we're in the same family record book, which means that our family model is recognized by the State.

And if I talk to you about "family symbolism"...

The notion of family is changing. The anti-marriage pour tous demonstrators thought that the family consisted of a mom, dad and children. But I know a lot of people like me who have two moms or two dads.

So, what does a family mean to you?

Parents who love, educate and protect one or more children, whether biological or adopted. It doesn't matter whether there are parents or just one. A family is above all about love, shared trust and, most importantly, dialogue...

How are things going with your mothers' respective families?

It took a while for my biological mother to introduce my other mother to her parents and, in the end, there were no problems. On the other hand, my other mom met girls quite young, so her family knew about her homosexuality. Both sides are very tolerant, whether it's my uncles, my aunts, my cousins or even my grandparents.

Was your mothers' marriage important for your family, and for you in particular?

Yes, because it was a big step for my family and for all the people around us. Over two hundred people were present at the town hall. My biological mother gave a beautiful speech that really moved me. This marriage is the recognition of our family by the State. That's no mean feat!

Do you feel you live in an unusual family?

Absolutely not! I have many friends who are in the same situation as me, or even in more "complicated" families. For example, I know a boy who has two fathers and two mothers, and a girl whose father and mother are now with a man and a woman respectively.

Do these situations make you feel personally richer?

Of course, especially from a personal point of view. Meeting all these people and growing up in my family has opened my eyes to all

4. Interview with Elsa, 20

kinds of families. However, I can't compare myself with the person I would have been if I'd been born into a traditional family, with a father and a mother. Quite simply, having lived with all kinds of families and being a leftist, I'm one of those people who's open-minded.

Have the latest "debates" on PMA made you feel concerned?

More than that: I'm flabbergasted that people refuse to understand that two moms and two dads are just as good as one mom and one dad. What's more, all the effort homosexual couples have to make to have children proves their real desire to have children and start a family, which, I think, guarantees as much as possible the love that will be given within their family. Heterosexual couples, on the other hand, often end up as parents without having really sought it out or wanted it.

Still today?

Yes. The proof is that they blame others.

What do you mean?

On the streets of Paris, I see a lot of tags saying, "I lack nothing, except a father. PMA without a father, endless pain." Nonsense! I never lacked anything in my fatherless family! I grew up very well surrounded, I'm very much loved by both my moms and I have a little sister whom I love dearly. Do the people who write this think they're putting themselves in the shoes of children born into families like mine? They are mistaken. I wouldn't wish for anything in the world to be born again into a family with a father and a mother. I thank my mothers for having me born into their family. The people who are bent on opposing PMA want to deprive wonderful people of having children and becoming great parents. They've lost their battle; we'll never give up ours.

5.
Alex, aged 22

I'm a geology student in Lyon, where I live with two small cats and my partner. I spend my days between classes, hobbies and commitments (lots of reading, video games, and my LGBTQIA+ association, arcENSiel de l'ENS). I was biologically conceived by my two parents, Nathalie and Franck. They met in the course of their work - they were researchers at the same place - and had two children: my little sister, two years my junior, and me.

When I was four, we left Holland, where my parents were doing their post-doctorate. Shortly afterwards, they separated because they didn't love each other anymore. I think my mother had always wanted to have children, but not necessarily to raise them as a couple. She wanted to raise them on her own, and already had a clear idea of how she wanted to raise her children. This too may have played a part in the separation. Some time later, both my parents were reunited with their current spouses. My mother met a woman, Marie, who became my second mother; and my father also met a woman, Sophie, with whom he had a third child whom I consider my brother and whom I adore.

At first, the change was a bit difficult. My parents worked out an amicable custody arrangement, with my father picking us up one day a week. At the time, my father lived with a friend in a shared apartment. It wasn't an ideal setting for us. It was a period of great strain on our relationship. Even when he met another woman and found a more stable life, he was never very involved in our upbringing. When he welcomed us, he wanted to make the most of our presence, so it was a bit like going to a friendly uncle's house. On the agenda: TV and Nutella! As we've grown up, we've managed to find more in common, and we get on better now that I'm an adult.

On the parental side, as soon as my mother met Marie, my sister and I adopted the newcomer. She quickly understood that my mother needed her own space as a mother, that she needed to educate us on her own. So she never tried to dominate our upbringing. I think that's what attracted us too: because she didn't try to take over, we sought her attention, her validation, and we quickly became attached to her. She's a very likeable person, a bit of a deadpan and always humorous. I have fond memories of my childhood with her. She was a history-geography teacher, and my mother a teacher of Earth Sciences. Both of them were keen to give us a well-rounded education, perhaps a little strict at times, but always very playful.

I remember making a model of the Château de Versailles with Marie, and building a fortified castle out of toilet paper rolls (a real fortified castle, mind you, with moats, high castle and low castle!), for my history-geography lessons. My moms were always very inventive when it came to teaching. For example, my mother wanted to give us a somewhat musical education. Instead of forcing us to listen to the classics, she bought us two notebooks. So, when she played us a piece of classical music, we had to write down what the music evoked in us and the emotions it provoked. That's how we discovered Vivaldi and Chopin!

*

To me, Marie is a mother. I'm very close to her, closer than I am to my stepmother on my father's side, for example, with whom I have a cordial relationship. I know that if my father were to separate from my stepmother, we might lose touch. Marie, on the other hand, means a lot to me. I consider her a parental figure. She raised me in the same way as my mother, since she's been there, in my home, every day since I was six. She's influenced my values, my behavior... sometimes even the expressions I use! So, for me, she's a mother. A second mother, in fact.

More than the biological dimension, it was the way my mothers raised us that created this slight difference. My biological mother was very present, often emotional. As a result, she's the person I love most in the world, apart from my little sister, and with whom I've also had the most conflicts. Indeed, every little point where I felt she was disappointed in me hurt so much that her opinion meant so much to me. I don't have this tumultuous relationship with Marie. Marie calms conflicts and, because she hasn't been as involved in our upbringing, my little sister and I have had fewer stumbling blocks with her. For example, she wasn't the one we negotiated with to go out or get a new phone! But that doesn't mean she's any less important. On the other hand, she doesn't want to be called "Mom". I think she'd be afraid of "stealing her place" from my biological mother. So we call her Marie, even though she considers us to be her children... in her own way!

On my father's side, when my stepmother arrived, she tried to play the role of mother, imposing her authority. For example, my father let us watch certain films, which we were used to watching. When my stepmother arrived, she decided that these films were "not for children". This created a conflict with her, partly because she was breaking our traditions, and partly because we thought: "Hey,

5. Alex, aged 22

you're not our mother! Because Marie didn't do that, she gained a very important place in our lives. By not trying to be a mother, Mary created another place for herself. She invented a posture: neither father, nor mother, but a different parental figure, who does not confer the same functions, not the same roles, and who, nonetheless, filled an empty place whose contours she knew how to draw accurately and appropriately.

Indeed, for me, talking about parenthood is less about biology than about authority. When I was a child, authority was embodied by the person who set limits for me, some of which were necessary in the context of learning about society: at the dinner table, in encounters with adults, you had to behave according to certain codes. My mother built this framework. My father never tried to exercise any authority over us! And maybe that's why it was hard for us to think of him as a father. He was more like a nice godfather who passed everything on to you. Maybe it had something to do with the fact that he only saw us once a week, so he tried to be as nice as possible.

Authority was my mother's domain. She was the only one who issued punishments and rewards to teach us how to behave, so it was she alone whom we sometimes found too restrictive. For example, within the educational framework she wanted to give us, we weren't allowed to go out with friends very much. It was all about academic and behavioral excellence. My sister and I always had an average grade of 18.5, whether in junior high or high school. My mother kept a close eye on things, and Marie had a kind of implicit authority: with my sister, we were very attached to her judgment. As a result, even if she didn't explicitly set the rules, we knew her well enough to be careful not to disappoint her.

When we returned from Holland, we lived by the sea. We lived very comfortably. I went to public schools in junior high and high school. Inevitably, with parents working for the public sector! I took part in a number of teachers' demonstrations, growing up with "Sarko t'es foutu, la jeunesse est dans la rue[11]" T-shirts from the age of eight.

On the classroom side, I've always been very precocious and eager to learn. I think this was developed by my elementary school. I went to a Freinet school, whose pedagogy respects the rhythm and autonomy of the pupils. In the mornings in particular, we have times when we choose our activities. There are bins with worksheets for French, math and science. Students set themselves a program for the week ("I'm going to do so many math worksheets, so many French worksheets"), and each day they can choose to do a little bit of everything, the idea being to finish their program by the end of the week, when the teacher assesses them. I liked this way of working and it pushed me a lot, because I love learning.

When I arrived at college, I was very comfortable with my schooling. I went to the school in my neighborhood. It wasn't a difficult school, but it had a very diverse student body. At the time, to be in a good class, you had to take German as your first language in the sixth year and Latin in the fifth. So that's what I did, and as I was very bored at the time, I also asked to take Italian with the Centre National d'Enseignement à Distance. In high school, I gave up German, passed an exam and entered the international Italian section. My high school was right on the beach - what a pleasure!

---

11. "Sarko you're screwed, the youth is in the street."

5. Alex, aged 22

The only drawback: at one point, my mother was my main teacher. I didn't like that at all.

After graduating from high school, I wanted to get out of the house, because I wanted to get away from this very academic environment, I wanted to have my own life and discover other places. I found a preparatory class and a boarding school in Lyon. Preparatory classes were very hard, especially on my self-confidence. To make matters worse, I failed the entrance exam for the École Normale Supérieure, which I entered on the basis of my academic record. Now that I'm a Master 2 student, I'm starting to regain a bit of self-confidence, knowing that I'm doing well in what I do. And that's important.

The fact that I live with two moms has never been a secret. At least, I never hid it from my friends. In primary school, Marie would sometimes pick me up after school. No one dared ask me any questions! In junior high school, I went to the same school where Marie was a teacher, and she didn't want anyone to know. My moms come from a generation where discrimination against LGBTQIA+ people was rife. However, we didn't hide it either: once, we went on a school trip together, and it was Marie who accompanied me in the car in the morning. At the end of the board meeting, where I was a delegate, we left together. No, it wasn't a secret, but I didn't shout it from the rooftops, because it was their private life, just as I wouldn't have shouted that my father was heterosexual and who he was sleeping with...

As for me, I had no problem accepting my bisexuality. Even in elementary school, I was attracted to my best friend! Growing up with two women meant that I didn't think much about my sexual orientation: I just realized that I was attracted to girls *and* boys without worrying about it. I didn't put the term "bisexual" on it until the end of middle school, because before that, I didn't know there were several terms! For me, it was normal - at least my own norm.

In high school, there was the somewhat difficult period of "marriage for all", in 2015 (it was my ninth year). Many of my friends, like me, had inherited their political sensibilities from their parents. There were little debates about it. I felt a little embarrassed because, in the eyes of the idiots, I was illustrating their belief that the children of lesbians necessarily become *gay* or lesbian. In my class, there was a new kid who was all "Manif pour tous". He said that if he was *gay*, he'd either go to the doctor for treatment or commit suicide. I also remember one of our brief exchanges, unbelievable but true.

- On TV," this idiot trumpeted, "I saw that when two *gays* have a child, it has Down's syndrome.

- Tell me, have you ever been to an SVT class?

Add to that a pinch of: "God created Adam and Eve to have children together", and you get the picture. In three words: complicated to deal with. I felt insulted. I felt insulted. My moms too. I was angry. And I could see these people demonstrating to eradicate our way of life and deny our right to family happiness. At home, we talked about it freely. My moms were very clear and reassuring:

- Let them talk, they're idiots. In the end, we'll win and all will be forgotten. Just think about protecting yourself, and be yourself.

*

My family background had a big influence on my politicization. When you're a victim of discrimination, it's hard not to be politicized: you have to fight for your rights. Right from the start, I was obviously in favor of "marriage for all" and the protection of

LGBTQIA+ people, since I was concerned. On top of this was the heritage of my Italian grandfather, who came to France with his father during the Second World War. He was a worker at Renault, a union member and a communist, and he shared with me left-wing values such as the idea that work shouldn't just be used by capitalists, but by all the people in order to live, feed and look after themselves... It was something that spoke to me and made me want to get involved.

At ÉNS, I joined an LGBTQIA+ association, more to help others than to feel supported. As a bisexual, I dated mostly boys. So I haven't often been discriminated against because of that. My boyfriend and I pass for a heterosexual couple, so we haven't had any problems finding a place to live... even though I'm non-binary and he's cis. I take advantage of the misunderstanding to suffer very little discrimination. On the other hand, I have been subjected to insults and degrading remarks. For example, some women ask me to make trouples for fun with their husbands. I find it unpleasant, degrading and uncomfortable, but I don't consider this kind of "invitation" to be discrimination.

Biphobia isn't systemic. It's mostly homophobia with a few more specific characteristics, such as the fact that the heterosexual model is so ingrained in our minds that many bisexual women find it easier to date men. Bisexuals often force themselves to be in a heterosexual relationship and end up in complicated situations because of our heteropatriarchal model. The main oppression for bisexuals is society's pressure to be heterosexual... but in the end, *gays* and lesbians experience this oppression too.

From then on, getting involved has brought me a lot, if only because I'm obliged to learn about the issues affecting queer people every day, like when I run a workshop on state transphobia. I want to make things happen on my own level because it's important that we all have the same rights... and because I've realized that enforcing identical rights is not always an easy task. For example, since the law on "marriage for all", same-sex couples have the right to marry at the town hall, but in practice, many mayors refuse to celebrate these unions. Officially, the law guarantees access to healthcare, but we know that, for trans people, this right is just wishful thinking.

As a result, I'm less attached to the notion of "law" in the sense of "legislation" than to the idea of changing mentalities, particularly those of the people on whom we are sometimes dependent (doctor, teacher, decision-maker, etc.). The problem is that change requires a constant back-and-forth between the law and people's mentalities. Changes in mentality often lead to changes in the law, because when everyone starts to have an idea, it's easier for the government to pass laws; conversely, the law also leads to changes in mentality, because when something becomes legal, it becomes normal in people's minds and, as a result, more accepted. In the end, society progresses by constantly going back and forth between what people think and what is established in law.

Consequently, for me, it's important to work on these two aspects. For example, by enshrining in the law that transphobia is punishable, when we are faced with transphobia, we have a lever with which to lodge a complaint; except that, when we lodge a complaint, we find ourselves facing the police, who are also largely gangrened by transphobia... It's complicated, but it's something that needs to move forward simultaneously. We can't push society to evolve if, behind it, we don't have a law to back us up and say:

- Look, I have the right, it's written. Even if you're transphobic, you can't deny me that.

5. Alex, aged 22

Then it's up to us to call for legislation and say:

- Wait a minute, that's not written into the law, even though you can see that we all agree with the idea!

It's important to demand these rights, and to move society forward, so that there's a two-way street between rights and attitudes.

6.
Interview with Aurore, 20

Could you briefly introduce yourself?

My name is Aurore, I'm twenty, I do theater and I live in Strasbourg.

Can you tell me about how you were conceived?

I have a father and a mother. When I was four, they split up and my mother went to live with a woman. This woman became my mother, too, because she brought me up.

Was your father involved in your upbringing?

Yes, I lived with him every other week. The other week, I lived with my two mothers. When I was eighteen, my second mother adopted me.

How did you feel about the change?

It was very complicated when I was young, because I lived in a very middle-class neighborhood in Paris. It wasn't done at the time, so I didn't tell anyone until I was fifteen. My mother didn't dare talk about it either. Nobody in the neighborhood knew.

What about your family?

When the news broke, my grandparents took it very badly. With marriage for all, the situation calmed down. Then, when I grew up, I also decided that it would be different, that it wouldn't be so complicated for me because people have bad images of it. It happened gradually, when I was in high school and my sister, who is now twenty-four, was in her first year of medical school. She hadn't told her friends either. She started talking about it when I was in high school.

When did you start thinking of your second mother as your mother?
There were three phases. The first was when I didn't know, because my mother didn't tell me right away that she was his wife. At that point, I was very close to her. Then, when I was eight, I found out that they were in fact together. At that point, I hated my mother and my other mother, because I was angry with them for not telling me. And the third phase was when I decided that what I was doing to them was horrible and that I didn't have to hate them. When I entered high school, I started to get much closer to my other mother. I was sixteen when they got married and my mother's wife was able to adopt us.

How do you interpret your initial hostility to this change?
I remember trying to talk to people about it. Every time, my girl-friends would say: "Yuck, that's disgusting", and "Anyway, it's not possible, it doesn't exist, when you love a boy, you can't love a girl afterwards and you can't have children"... I heard horrible things. So I was kind of immersed in that.

Religion played its part too...
Yes. I come from a Jewish family where homoparenting isn't even imaginable. My father and mother are Jewish. I imagine it would have been the same with Catholics or Muslims...

What is your mothers' relationship with religion?

My biological mother is Jewish. She is more attached to tradition than to God, speaks Hebrew, has inherited a very heavy history and still bears the scars of the Shoah. The fact that she was a woman was very complicated for my grandparents. My mother's going out with a woman was unheard of in either religion or custom. For them, my mother's divorce was already a catastrophe, so when they found out she was living with a woman, it was too much, and the ties were broken. With time, I think they accepted it. At least, they stopped rejecting her. My other mother is an atheist. She's very interested in Judaism for its spiritual aspect, just as she is in Buddhism. It was sometimes complicated for her to be seen as the *goï*.

At the time, did you feel discriminated against, or was it rather through you that your mothers and possibly your father suffered?

Both of them! First of all, my parents were discriminated against because they weren't like all the other families in the school, which is quite a significant discrimination. As for me, we were suspicious because I had a girlfriend who told me one day that *it was* transmitted. She said to me: "But then, so are you...". When I was little, I was too afraid that my girlfriends would tell me they didn't want to be friends with me for that reason.

Have you felt concerned or involved by the debates of recent years, particularly around "marriage for all"?

When the debates around "marriage for all" began, I was in secondary school. Nobody knew about my situation. I was very involved and virulent, but nobody really understood why. It has to be said that both my mothers are doctors, so I've always been brought up with the idea that there's no reason why some people

59

can and others can't. But, for example, there's no reason why some people can't and others can. But, for example, there's something I've never understood: why are single women allowed to adopt, and two women not?

Yes, why do you think the state denies them this opportunity?
Because we're in a country with centuries of Christian values. So we're an ultraconservative country, whereas opening adoption up to homosexual couples would be a step forward.

How do you see the social situation of same-sex couples evolving?
I'm very optimistic. When I see my little sisters, mentalities have changed... They're in high school, they're much more open than we are, even with five years' difference: when I see their generation, I'm very optimistic about evolution, about body acceptance and the choice of love and the choice of one's body in general.

Can you think of any rights that same-sex families have yet to win?
I don't really know what's forbidden in same-sex families, because I still had a father, so we had access to all the rights of hetero-parenthood.

I forgot to ask you what this father figure means to you... Did you feel you lacked a male figure, as opponents of lesboparental families claim?
It's funny, because it was my father, who worked in perfumes, who taught me how to put on make-up, how to dress, how to put on nail varnish - everything that, in a way, is "not masculine". Of course, he's a man, so I imagine there was something different about his upbringing. For all that, my father doesn't brandish his masculinity

as a banner, he doesn't shout: "I'm the father, so you listen to me."
I was lucky to live with three human beings who loved me.

How do you view the distribution of gender roles in your family constellation? Between your two mothers, in particular?

My biological mother doesn't do much at home. She does a lot, but not when it comes to cooking, housework… Not because she's lazy, just because her education is lacking. For example, she doesn't know how to cook. The idea of cooking really scares her. So my other mother took care of that, as well as all the household chores. It was less a question of distribution than of character. For example, my mother, who likes to organize papers, took care of the taxes. One of us is more athletic than the other, so we did more sporting activities with her, and so on.

Thanks to your experience, do you feel you have a privileged opinion on parenthood and gender issues in general?

What my experience has taught me is that a lesboparental family is a happy one. My upbringing and our family structure are the last things in my life that could make me suffer. I suffered before when I was ashamed, but society has changed, mentalities, the way others look at things, everything has evolved in a direction that I find positive, at least on this subject.

Why?

When I was little, I used to hear: "They're going to go and see a shrink, they're not going to be well". I saw one every day, as my mother is a paedophile! Today, we know that children who suffer are not those who have received too much love because they have three parents, or because they were not raised with a male or

6. Interview with Aurore, 20

female figure. On the other hand, according to my mother, children need to know that, in order to exist, they need an ovum and a spermatozoon. Both my mothers taught me that it's good to be raised by two women and a man, and that the images we inherit of gender roles and the figures needed for a child's development need to be challenged.

7.
Léa, 23 years old

I'm an illegal child.

"Illegal" is the word the notary pronounced as he drew up my adoption deed, to describe the way my mothers gave birth to me. Illegal? What good news! I was 16 at the time, and delighted to be able to add a *badass* adjective to my identity. My mothers had braved both frontiers and the law to create me - wasn't that the most beautiful proof of love? I had been so desired, and now I was loved, supported and protected!

Laurence and Nathalie met in 1991, both working for La Poste in the Paris region. Their relationship provoked a variety of reactions in their respective families, but they were able to build on the support they received. After a few years, like many couples, they felt the desire to have a child. Since, for them, having a child is not as simple as the heterosexual act commonly known as "coitus", they opted for artificial insemination by anonymous donor in the Netherlands, on the advice of APGL, an essential - if not the only - source of information available in the pre-Internet era. This choice corresponded to their imagination and to the family culture they were shaping. Their desire was to have recourse to a medically supervised act of donation that would give their child a founding narrative made up of three entities: mom, Nata, and someone-good. This donor only enters the story of my conception for the duration of a disinterested act. He left my parents with the emotional role, the desire, the education - in short, the role of "parent". As I grew up, my parents were able to tell me our story in the right words. So I was able to love it, accept it and, today, consider it a source of pride.

In the small town in the Vendée where I grew up, our family always aroused a little benevolent curiosity, a great deal of acceptance. We've always felt normal in the local landscape. We laugh together at the surprise of their co-workers as well as at the questions and concerns of the school staff. My oldest friends and cousins grew up "knowing" and seeing lesboparenting as a normal family pattern.

Yet in France, this family pattern only became legal in May 2013. A few months later, my mothers got married after 22 years together. More than an occasion to celebrate, it was a chance for Nathalie to be officially recognized as my legal parent. It didn't change anything in my daily life; I simply added her matronym to that of Laurence. Nathalie had been present at my birth; she picked me up from school, took me to the doctor, signed my correspondence books and did all those everyday things you do when raising a child. Her legal non-recognition was only felt when an official signature was required, which is relatively rare. However, my mother's loyalty and benevolence alone ensured that she retained and exercised her parental authority in all circumstances. I can imagine that some unacknowledged parents may find themselves separated from their child as a result of death or family upheaval. My adoption was therefore mainly symbolic, without changing our daily lives, but it was an important recognition for the three of us.

For me, my normality is self-evident. But now I'm waiting for the authorities to adapt to our family pattern and for people's consciences to calm down. In 2020, I'm still entering Nathalie's name in the "father" box on many administrative documents. When I was applying for a visa to study in Brazil, the ambassador himself had to rule on the presence of a female first name in the "padre" box. I hope one day to see the legality of my family recognized in official documents. As a child, having my voice heard is a privilege that I hope will make people realize that my family situation is not a handicap, but rather a strength and a source of pride. I understand and respect the fact that some people, because of their cultures and beliefs, don't understand lesboparenting. I'm not asking them to come to Gay Pride, but simply to keep their convictions in their private sphere, since the shape of my family in no way affects their daily lives. I believe that words and education are tools that can help us build a respectful and tolerant society.

That's why I'm sharing my story. My "normality" is a gift that I hope will bring more understanding and less hatred. If I could choose, I would choose again to grow up in my family, loved and wanted; I feel neither lack nor pain, only love and the sensation of having acquired a great openness of mind.

*

The terms "homosexuality" and "heterosexuality" refer to the sexual preferences of individuals. They are two ends of a spectrum that today includes many other forms of sexual orientation: bisexuality, pansexuality, asexuality and so on. These terms are often part of an individual's identity. They are used to reflect the difference between a sexual orientation and a norm. Who identifies as heterosexual before being confronted with another orientation? Words are therefore tools for asserting one's identity, asserting oneself and finding sexual partners.

7. Léa, 23 years old

From the very beginning of my life, I've been in contact with both homosexual and heterosexual couples. Growing up, I was always asked:

- Do you have a boyfriend or girlfriend?

By giving me the choice, my moms and family told me that the gender or sex of the person who would share my life didn't matter to them. Their language and recurrent contact with different types of couple led me never to prioritize different types of sexuality. So I don't put my own sexual orientation into words, just as I don't put others' into words. I'm surprised when some of my interlocutors make a subject of it. I rationally understand the need for identification and the desire to name different sexualities, but I don't emotionally grasp the meanings of these terms. Perhaps this is the culmination of the normalization of varied sexual orientations within our society: no longer noticing differences based on a supposed norm. For me, the normalization of different types of sexuality will be accomplished when it is no longer a subject.

*

We use language to represent our environment and bring it into existence. Naming the things that surround us means recognizing their public existence and including them in our world. When we depict the birth of language in a child, we often show that the first words will be used to designate his or her parents: most often "mom" and "dad". These terms are used to name the most important people in a child's life. They are only used by siblings to refer to their parents, who will change their names when talking about their parents to people outside the nuclear family. We'll use "ma maman", "ma mère", "mon papa", "mon père", and the outsider will understand that the speaker is talking about his or her parents.

Children from lesboparental families also need to name their environment, but are faced with the non-existence of pre-established language terms to designate their parents. The term "mom" is naturally used in some families, including my own, to designate the biological and parental mother. But how can we designate the non-biological mother without repeating the term "maman", which would make it impossible to distinguish the two individuals, or the term "papa", normally associated with a masculine identity?

In my family, the importance of naming met a practical need for identification. Finding a name for my non-biological but oh-so-so-so-social mother included her in the nuclear family and gave her a role. So I call my second parent "Nata". Her first name is "Nathalie", she prefers to be called "Nat" by those around her, and I'm the only one who calls her Nata. I use this term when I speak to her, or when I talk about her to a third person from my family circle. When I talk about her to someone outside my family circle, I use "Nathalie". For me, it has the same function as "my mother", since it doesn't include the affective nickname, and allows me to talk about my parents in a more detached and mature way than when I use a term like "my mom". In this way, the dichotomy between "Nata" and "Nathalie" allows me to bring my non-biological relative into existence through naming.

It fills the void of language, but has a limit: it's my own. It is not understood by newcomers and constantly requires introduction and explanation. When I want to talk about Nathalie to people unfamiliar with my family's peculiarities, a number of situations arise. To avoid explanation, I sometimes use the all-encompassing term "my parents". At other times, I use "my mother", even though

7. Léa, 23 years old

I'm referring to Nathalie because she is legally called mother; she wouldn't like to know that I use this term to refer to her on rare occasions, since she doesn't identify with it and claims both her name and her special place. Nevertheless, it allows me to maintain a conversation without explaining my family situation - not that it would be awkward, but it might bring some people into an intimacy or knowledge of me that I don't wish to invite them into.

However, I've never hidden the fact that I have two mothers. This was never a problem. It was even a strength during my teenage years, as it enabled me to build up a public image that was considered *cool* even though I felt shy. The reaction of my interlocutors can be summarized in three ways:

- curiosity about my conception, the way others see me, my feelings, and even my own sexuality;

- the delay effect - no immediate reaction, then lots of questions; and

- non-reaction.

Non-reaction can be a sign of modesty or distance, but it can also be a sign that my family situation is becoming more and more commonplace and accepted. I don't mind reactions. Answering questions allows me to educate my interlocutors. Educating and informing them enables them to understand and then accept. I've never had to deal with hatred linked to my family situation - where else could it come from? On the other hand, I've always wanted to destroy the prejudices that see my family as false and unhealthy.

*

Language is important every day, not just in terms of who raises me, but also in my conception of my family. My parents have always referred to the person who provided the sperm for my conception as a "donor".

This term is fraught with meaning and symbolism, both in what it represents and in what it does not. It means that I was conceived by someone anonymous to me, without identity, and from whom I have nothing to expect. People sometimes ask me if I feel the lack of a father. I think we run the risk of feeling a lack if we build up an imaginary father who, of course, can't meet our expectations. The use of the word donor doesn't allow me to feel a lack, I don't have any emotions towards this person apart from gratitude. The choice my parents made enabled them to build me a full and sufficient family representation made up of two loving people. I have no social or emotional expectations of a "father" who doesn't exist; I had Nata and a mother who are fully sufficient for me.

So, for me, the formation of a lesboparental family within a heteronormative patrilineal society requires the invention of new terms to enrich the collective imagination and meet the needs of the child. These bricolages are precious. They allow us to convey love, to feel normal, and to live a peaceful daily life. The right definition of the non-biological parent and the sperm donor are, for me, the two keys to a child's equilibrium. These are just two words, so easy and natural to install, that provide the child with a stable framework and normal development. That's my answer to all the questions other people ask: don't worry about me, my parents gave me the two words of stability.

Interlude
The story of Mathilde, 23

Interlude

July 2007. In Saintes-Maries-de-la-Mer

This is the second summer we've gone on vacation without our fathers. The moms have rented a large pitch at a campsite with a swimming pool, a ten-minute walk from the beach. At the far end of our large patch of parched grass, we've set up two tents. One for each sibling. The caravan reserved for the moms is stationed at the entrance to the site.

"Moms. Among children, that's what we call them. We never mention our fathers. "Dads": impossible plural. We've never seen them with each other, so we can't imagine that expression. During those two weeks at sea, neither the kids nor the moms talk about them. By the Mediterranean, fathers disappear.

*

At Saintes-Maries, there are lots of earwigs.

Quentin, Éli, Johann, Zoé and I debate their name: is it *earwig* or *earwig*? We look closely at the insects and decide, from their sharp mandibles, that they are indeed earwigs.

*

One night, my sister, my brother and I are lying in our tent. Zoé complains of thirst. Johann turns on the flashlight to look for our water bottle. The light casts pale rays on the white canvas. Zoé squeals: dozens of earwigs have invaded the tent. The panicking insects run in all directions across the canvas, right above us. We rush out of the tent.

Outside, it's cold. In search of shelter, we knock on the caravan door. Maman and Isabelle open the door, their tousled hair falling back on their summer pyjamas. All around them, the smell of sleep. We tell them about our misadventure. Isabelle becomes exasperated. Mom says nothing. Usually, children aren't allowed in the caravan. They let us in anyway, and offer to let us sleep in the smaller of the two beds in the caravan.

I'm surprised to see that the sheets line the mattress. Every morning, the two beds and their sheets are a mess. But tonight, the cot is still made up. I sneak a peek at Mum and Isabelle, their pyjamas rumpled. They slept in the same bed. Is it like this every night? Why do they undo the second bed in the morning?

For the first time, I wonder if moms are lying to us. If they're in love.

*

The next day, Quentin and Éli laugh loudly at our scare during the earwig invasion. Isabelle adds:

- Those bugs are nothing, get used to them!

All three of them offend me enough for me to forget my doubts about Mama and Isabelle's love.

*

When we return, we don't even think of asking our father what he did while we were at sea. Nor do we tell him about our vacation. As if the reunion would erase those two weeks. Or as if those vacations were from another time. A shard of the future, chipping away at the present, vainly masking the burrs of the lie.

February 2008. On the way home from school

MATHILDE

Oh, I forgot to tell you, my parents are getting divorced!

IRIS

I don't believe you. If you did, you would have told me this morning.

MATHILDE

I swear!

IRIS

Then why didn't you say so as soon as we met?

MATHILDE

I'd forgotten.

IRIS

I can't believe your parents are getting divorced: you're the most perfect little family I've ever met!

*

My mother is a translator. She decided to devote herself fully to raising her children after the birth of her second baby. The house is always clean and tidy. Once her children have grown up and are all at school, my mother starts giving a few English lessons at private language centers or youth clubs, just to keep herself busy.

She doesn't need to earn a lot of money: my father is an engineer. He works for a company specializing in biomechanics, something to do with robots. I don't quite understand what he does, but he works a lot, often goes to Paris during the week, and always comes home late at night.

My brother is in ninth grade. My little sister is still at elementary school. We live in a big, two-storey house surrounded by a garden. When he's here in the evening, my father waters his flowers. In summer, when it's hot, he installs an inflatable pool that can't compete with our neighbors' in-ground pools, but where we can still invite them to swim.

*

"The perfect little family." The phrase runs through my head. Not the words. More the slight contempt in Iris's voice.

March 2008

One evening when Dad was away, I opened my bedroom door, slipped into the hallway and descended the first flight of stairs. Through the bars of the banister, I see Isabelle in the living room. She's lying on the sofa. Her two feet, open like a duck, rest on the coffee table.

I climb the stairs as quietly as possible.

April 2008

MATHILDE

Zoé, we have to go and tell Mom that, even if she's a lesbian, we'll always love her.

ZOÉ

What does "lesbian" mean?

MATHILDE

She's a girl who likes girls.

ZOÉ

Yuck.

MATHILDE

But if Mom was a lesbian, you'd still love her, right?

ZOÉ

Yes, it's Mom.

MATHILDE

So we'll tell him. Just in case. So she'll dare to tell us.

June 2008

MOM

When school starts, I'll be moving to a new house. You'll come every other week. It shouldn't be too difficult for you to adapt to the house, since you already know it: it's Quentin and Éli's house.

MATHILDE

I knew it!

ZOÉ

But we... We're not getting a new house, so... We already know this one... It's a shame... Will we still be able to choose the color of our bedroom walls?

MOM

Yes... Maybe... I don't know... I don't want to promise you anything, I'm... I'm really sorry...

ZOÉ

Why are you sad, Mom?

MOM

I feel like I've missed everything in my life...

MATHILDE

Well, not everything! Look: you didn't miss us.

MOM

Thanks, sweetheart. Please don't say anything to Quentin and Éli just yet.

MATHILDE

Why?

MOM

They don't know yet. Isabelle will tell them just before the vacations. We had decided to tell you before, but every time, Isabelle puts it off, she doesn't dare... I couldn't lie to you anymore. And then I thought I'd better tell you, because now Dad too...

JOHANN, incredulous

Dad too is...

MOM

No, he's not! Dad's not gay. He too has met another woman...

In front of the sea, rocks lean against the embankment covered in dry, yellowing grass that separates the beach from the parking lot.

MATHILDE

And there we are! We're on top of the rocks!

ÉLI

It's a great hiding place. They won't find us here.

(Long silence.)

ÉLI

It's weird, us living together.

MATHILDE

Yes.

QUENTIN

Don't you think being gay is a bit of a disease?

MATHILDE

But no!

QUENTIN

And, first of all, we brought you everything. The house we're all going to live in was ours first. The places we go on vacation, it was our mother who showed them to yours. We even used to go with our father! And all the friends they see are our parents' friends. Because your mother doesn't have any friends.

MATHILDE

N'importe quoi! You wouldn't even know where Holland was if our mother wasn't Dutch.

(Silence again. We play with the sand caught in the rocks).

QUENTIN

That may be so. But without us, you'd have nothing at all.

December 2009. In Figeac

Every year, on the morning of December 25, the youngest cousin places the baby Jesus in the crib. The santons Joseph and Mary watch over him. Papi then gives each of his four sons a calendar for the coming year. Twelve family photos illustrate the twelve months, topping a full-page grid of days. Birthday days are recalled by the insertion of small individual portraits, between the empty squares of daily life.

In 2010, Mom's face disappears.

I look carefully at the calendar. Our cousins' mothers are still smiling, neatly arranged in their birthday boxes. But Mom is gone. Her face has crossed the thin barricades that criss-cross the square days. She has fled the white squares of April. And the inscription "Maman Marieke" has replaced her photo.

I can hear the baby Jesus giggling in his corner. Joseph, looking on, is his father. Because there has to be one. And, since children also need a mother, "Maman Marieke" occupies the slot for his birthday. But her face is erased. Like the dead, whose features we can't quite make out.

*

"Mama Marieke".

As far as the family story is concerned, Marieke is now just the mother of her children.

I wonder if it's his homosexuality that's disturbing.

*

Isabelle and my mother live at 31 allée des Fresnes, my father at 19 rue du Vallon. Isabelle had invented this encrypted code, so that we didn't have to say "chez papa" and "chez maman", but felt at home everywhere. My mother was quick to adopt the simple expression "chez papa". My father, on the other hand, never stopped saying 31.

At first, when he talked about my mother, he'd say "mom". Then the possessive "ta" crept in. Gradually, "maman" became "ta maman". A possessive adjective that joined me to her and separated my parents. And soon Paul Hoetzel simply referred to Marieke Meijer as "le 31". And so, in my father's language, the mother of his children slowly faded away.

January 2010

When I get back to 31, I ring the bell to get someone from inside to open the door for me. The lock is always turned. The kids don't have the keys.

Isabelle and my mother are in the living room. As soon as I enter, I give them the second of the day's three ritual kisses, along with the morning one to say hello and the evening one before bed.

Maman and Isabelle also kiss each other. They don't kiss in front of us either. In the morning, when Mum leaves for work, Isabelle meets her in the hall. From the kitchen, we can hear the light snap of their kiss. We never see anything more.

When I kiss them, I always start with Isabelle. That way, I can wash my cheeks against my mother's when I kiss her back. If that's not enough, I go into the bathroom to rinse my face. When I lock the door, I hold back the handle. If I don't, the lock clicks, and this noise disturbs Isabelle, who's watching TV.

Then I go to the kitchen. I'm a bit hungry. In the big drawer, there's a packet of cakes. I have to ask permission to eat them first. I return to the living room, a packet under my arm, and look furtively at my reflection as I pass in front of the mirror.

ISABELLE

Yes, yes, you're pretty.

MATHILDE, to Mama, showing the package

May I?

MOM

Yes.

ISABELLE

You should be careful, Mathilde. You're only eleven, you haven't got a woman's body yet, so you can eat as much sugar as you like without gaining an ounce. But, as soon as you've had your period... that'll all be over!

Back to the kitchen. Eat my cakes anyway. Then back to the red room, with the suitcase I drag from house to house every Wednesday. Even with the door closed, I can hear the endless chatter of Isabelle's TV.

I have to empty the suitcase and, for a week, try to settle in.

*

By the 31st, I'm bumping into walls, chairs, doorknobs and missing stairs. This house hates me.

At night, before falling asleep, I think of Isabelle. I imagine her falling to the bottom of the hole dug in the garden by the workmen installing the swimming pool. I see piles of earth tumbling down on top of her.

*

The week passes slowly.

*

I celebrate my return to the 19. There, I keep my room, the shower is not compulsory and, sometimes, Sabine comes to eat with us.

The first evening she came home for dinner, Dad had asked us to prepare a grapefruit salad as a starter. Sabine didn't know how to cut these citrus fruits, remove their little white skins without bursting the pulp, or prepare the mayonnaise to accompany them.

To make sure Dad found what he'd expected in the bowl, I tried to show Sabine how Mom peeled grapefruit. She removed all the skins, even the most transparent ones, and served us the citrus fruit in regular, translucent, shiny pieces. Perfect grapefruit. One day, Isabelle told her it was a waste of time, and now Mum just cuts the fruit into two hemispheres. We eat them by digging into our citrus half with a teaspoon, just like at the canteen.

That evening, Sabine and I tried hard to cut the grapefruit the way Mom used to, but we just couldn't do it. Under our hands, the fruit shredded into senseless pieces.

A little ashamed, we served Dad our pinkish mashed potatoes. We laughed nervously, like friends, as we brought the bowl over.

February 2010. By car

MOM

Mathilde, before we get home, I've got to tell you... You've got to be more careful what you say. Yesterday afternoon, you said something that Isabelle didn't like at all.

MATHILDE

Really? What did I say?

MOM

That Sabine was like a friend to you.

MATHILDE

And she's jealous?

MOM

Not at all, but she believes that children can't be friends with adults.

October 2011

IRIS

It's funny. You always say "my parents" when talking about your father and your stepmother.

MATHILDE

Yes, because it's quicker than saying "my father and my stepmother" all the time. Besides, I don't like the word "stepmother", it sounds like a Disney villain.

IRIS

What about your mother?

MATHILDE

Well, I say "they".

IRIS

And if, one day, she finds a boyfriend, what will you do?

MATHILDE

There's no risk.

IRIS

Oh, isn't she sad to be all alone when your father has found someone?

MATHILDE

No. It's not in her plans to find a boyfriend. She wants to spend time with her best friend.

IRIS

Quentin's mother? The one who lives downstairs from you?

MATHILDE

Downstairs at my mother's, yes.

December 2011

MATHILDE

Isabelle, why don't you want us to tell our friends the truth? Our closest friends, the ones we trust... I'm sure my friends would keep it to themselves, if I asked them to.

ISABELLE

It can't be done. It's too big. It's too big a secret. No one can keep it to themselves.

MATHILDE

There are plenty of people who already suspect it, and are talking about it! Why pretend? By continuing to lie, we give the impression that homosexuality must be hidden, and...

ISABELLE

By coming out openly, we run the risk of being rejected. Our society is still very homophobic.

MATHILDE

Someone has to take that risk for society to evolve!

ISABELLE

That's easy for you to say. You're surrounded by good friends. That's not the case for me or Quentin. And you're the only one of the kids who's willing to talk about it. Quentin doesn't want anyone to know. If you talk about it, you'll be relieved, but the other four will be very uncomfortable. So it's fairer for everyone to keep quiet.

*

Between children, before divorces, we used to say "moms".

Then we lived together, and separated them. There was "my mother and yours", "mom and Isabelle", "their mother and ours".

To others - my friends, my father's family, people I met on a daily basis - I would say "they", taking advantage of the inaudible plural to respect the imposed rule of silence, while telling the truth. I was experimenting with honesty through lies. The twisted presence of the *s* at the end of the word lifted my pride in myself, while in the silence of this letter, I kept the promise made to mothers to speak only of "her".

The others had funny ways of talking about Isabelle and my mother. During family gatherings, a paternal uncle would discreetly ask me:

- And how are they doing at Mom's?

I replied:

- *They're* fine.

MATHILDE

... and so I ask my mother if I can go out, and she tells me she has to talk to Isabelle first before giving me an answer. So, from that moment on, I know it's going to be a no and that, once again, I won't be allowed.

IRIS

But, Mathilde... Are you sure your mother and Isabelle aren't together?

MATHILDE, *blowing*

Thank you for finally asking the question. Of course they're together!

IRIS

Ah, I was thinking, too...

(Silence.)

IRIS

Why didn't you tell me?

MATHILDE

No right.

IRIS

And why do you -

MATHILDE

I had no right to say it, but I don't have to lie. Now that you've asked me directly, I can tell you the truth.

IRIS

Are you going to get yelled at?

Mathilde, *shrugging her shoulders*

I don't care. I'll tell them I missed it, or that I couldn't lie to you.

(Silence.)

Iris

Didn't you have the right to talk about it?

Mathilde

No.

Iris

Why?

Mathilde

Quentin doesn't accept that his mother is a lesbian. It's bad enough he can't handle his parents' divorce, but you can imagine… What's more, Isabelle can't handle it either, supposedly because she's a substitute teacher.

Iris

And?

Mathilde

She's afraid that the other teachers will say about her: "Well, there goes the Goudou substitute". And since Quentin and I went to the same school, I wasn't allowed to talk about it around me.

Iris

Even to me?

Mathilde

No, not to anyone.

Iris

Wait, there's something I don't understand. Quentin, he's *gay,* right?

Precisely. Before, he was afraid that people at our college would say: "Like mother, like son". I thought that, in high school, at least I'd be able to talk, I'd be liberated. You bet... We're still in the same school. I'm going to have to keep lying to everyone... It's already starting. When I introduce myself to people I don't know, they ask me questions: "Hi, what do your parents do, and where do they live, ah right they're divorced, and have they remarried? Ah, your father yes, but your mother no, poor thing, it can't be easy for her..." I've had enough of this!

Iris

Frankly, you should insist on being allowed to talk about it. Besides, now you can tell them that I know, and that I don't really care, that your mother is a lesbian.

*

I'm so relieved. When Iris finally asked me if my mother and Isabelle were a couple, my shoulders relaxed, as if I'd just released a small animal with wrinkled, dirty, peeling skin, the child of a dog and a rat, after years of holding it to my chest. Falling at my feet, the little animal ran away. It disappeared in a patch of sunlight, between the shadows of the square where Iris and I were chatting.

*

I want to talk.

Telling the story of my mother who crashes and ruins us with her, when Quentin and Éli laugh at her clumsiness, and Isabelle takes her snide look with them.

Evoking the evenings when I'd fall asleep with the image of Isabelle falling into the deep hole in the pool, dug between the stumps of the tall, dead cherry trees where, as children, we'd climb.

To denounce the seduction operation lurking behind that blue pool, to say loud and clear that the smoke and mirrors wouldn't fool me. That I wouldn't let myself be fooled by the reflections of family happiness on the surface of the artificial pool. That it wouldn't make me love Isabelle.

I want to share out loud my regret at not having had, on my mother's side, a stepmother other than this woman I detest.

I want to explain to my friends why I can't invite them home.

I want to describe my mother's weakness, powerless to convince Isabelle that Johann, Zoé and I are also at home at 31, and that Quentin and Éli shouldn't have any more rights there than we do.

I want to denounce the little injustices of everyday life. To tell them so that others share my hatred.

I want to talk to escape.

But I say nothing. And, since I can't put Isabelle through the tribunal of my inclinations, I start running away from everything intangible and invasive about her. Her perfume, her voice, the sound of her footsteps on the stairs. All that her passage leaves in the places she crosses. I flee the invisible imprints of her presence. I escape the stain of her proximity without letting on that it's her I'm avoiding. I don't read the books in her library, so that my eyes don't follow the lines of ink stained by her gaze. At the breakfast table, so I don't have to look at her, I line up milk cartons and cereal packets. I set up barricades against which my gaze stumbles. The cornflakes ingredient list becomes more familiar than her face.

The lies torment me all the more because I'd like to take pride in my special mother and my weird family. To score points with my artist friends who despise normality. I want to be that remarkable girl who embraces the fact that she has a lesbian mother. I want to tell the truth to compensate for the pain of living with Isabelle with the aura that my mother's strangeness would give me.

*

One day, my mother confided in me that she too would prefer to tell the truth. But Isabelle refuses, so we stick to the lie. In this small town on the outskirts of Montpellier, gossip spreads fast. Isabelle is afraid of other people, of the way they look at her. She's convinced that the women she refers to as "Radio Montpellier" are peering in through the window, then peddling the secrets of their spied-on neighbors.

*

And then, one day, that's it, I wrest from my mother and Isabelle the right to confess to the others that I lied to them. I finally tell them about the 31st. I talk about what's wrong. Isabelle's jealousy, the gradual suffocation of the complicity between my mother and me. The end of our nothing-but-with-each-other. I recall the time when Mom and I would repeat the word "charbon" together, ten, twenty, thirty times in a row, until we lost all meaning and laughed ourselves silly. I tell my friends how these little games died out under Isabelle's reproving sighs.

I describe the shelter from the 19th after the week to the 31st.

Immediately, questions, opinions and advice pour in. Why doesn't your mother tell his wife? Why are you going back? You should stay with your father and Sabine, if you're better off there!

At first, I answered sincerely. Then, little by little, I became afraid. It's a time when opponents of gay marriage are taking to the streets and billboards. What if some of them hijacked my story? What if they used it to illustrate the toxicity of lesboparenting?

I backtrack and say that from now on, everything's fine between Isabelle and me. Unlike the lie of the early years, I talk about my mother-in-law and keep quiet about the executioner.

February 2013

When I refer to Isabelle as "my mother's girlfriend", I watch out for the eyebrows and frowns of my interlocutors. The first few times, I justify myself by explaining that my mother has a girlfriend, not a boyfriend, but she assumed she was a lesbian after her marriage to my father, which is why she had children, including me.

Hence: my mother's girlfriend.

Reactions vary.

- Say, your family is complicated!

- So *cool* to have a lesbian mom!

- But really, is your mother bi or gay?

- And how did she find out?

There are also people who don't react. They wait for me to finish my sentence and keep a straight face when I talk about Isabelle.

With time, I stop watching faces and justifying myself as soon as an eyebrow furrows. If a question comes up, I simply answer that I have two mothers-in-law: Sabine, my paternal mother-in-law, and Isabelle, my maternal mother-in-law.

DAD

Today, *the* big problem facing society when it comes to bringing up children is that there's no longer a masculine figure for little boys to identify with.

MATHILDE

What do you mean?

SABINE

Well, people who make cartoons, for example, no longer dare invent male heroes because they're afraid of being accused of machismo.

DAD

Yes, just look at the latest Disney characters. They're all girls!

MATHILDE

Yeah, I mean, have you seen what Disney princesses look like? I'm a girl, and I don't want to look like them.

SABINE

But at least it shows that women can be heroes. But at least it shows that women can be heroes, and sets an example for little girls. Whereas, for boys, there's no role model at all.

DAD

And not just in Disney! It's much more general. We're experiencing a crisis of masculinity.

SABINE

And that's problematic, because little boys need male heroes to identify with...

DAD

... just as they need a mother and a father.

MATHILDE

Right?

Dad

Well, just read Rufo! He says that children need a mother figure *and* a father figure to have a balanced upbringing.

Mathilde

Nonsense! Have you ever asked children who have two moms or dads? They'll never tell you they're unbalanced because they have two parents of the same sex. I don't come from a same-sex family, but every other week I'm raised by two women. The rest of the time, by a man and a woman. You. I know both patterns, and I can tell you it's all the same.

Dad

I don't know... Maybe... It's true that, after what happened to me, maybe I'm neither very objective nor very open when it comes to homosexuality...

*

The status of the *paterfamilias* has been eroded, and all the better for it. There's more equality between the sexes.

I find the argument of my fellow psychoanalysts that you need a father and a mother curious, as if they both lived on a desert island, with no aunts, grandfathers or cousins? The father and mother are a mosaic, a multitude of maternal and paternal figures who come from elsewhere. What's more, I haven't seen anything unusual in homoparental families; they have the same difficulties as other families.

I'm against stigmatizing a population on the pretext that they have a different sexuality.

(Marcel Rufo, "Homoparentalité: au cœur du débat. Those who are "for",

in: Le Journal des femmes, January 29, 2013)

ZOÉ

Why did you tell Dad we didn't need a father figure? That's disgusting! It's like telling him we don't need him.

MATHILDE

No, I don't. What I meant was that it's not because he defines himself as a man that I consider him my father, but because he raised me. If he'd been a woman, I'd have loved him just as much.

Late November 2013

DAD

Here, we've left you all the documents we could find on the HPV vaccine... From your GP and pediatrician. It explains the advantages and the many disadvantages.

SABINE

We also got you some pro-vaccination *flyers*. They're published by the labs, but this way you'll know the arguments for and against, and can form your own opinion.

DAD

Take this, it's a letter you can give to Sabine's gynecologist when you go to see him. It just says that we're giving you permission to go alone. We've made an appointment for you next week.

MATHILDE

I'll be on 31.

DAD

It doesn't matter. Here's a letter you can give to the gynecologist. It authorizes you to consult on your own.

MOM

Wait, I don't understand why they don't want you to have this vaccine... I don't understand your father anymore. Before the divorce, when you needed to be vaccinated, he'd let me take care of it, I'd make an appointment for you with the doctor, and that was that... He never asked any questions. Since he's been with Sabine, he's changed so much! It's all become so complicated...

MATHILDE

But they're not the only ones saying it's better not to take this vaccine... Iris, too, says the labs created the vaccine just to make money...

MOM

Listen... for once we can protect ourselves against cancer...

ISABELLE

Your father never cared about your health. Mom has always looked after you on her own, and now, from one day to the next, he's meddling in your vaccinations! All he had to do was take an interest before.

MOM

And what's all this about Sabine's gynaecologist appointment? Do you want to see a gynecologist?

MATHILDE

Er... No, not really. It was to ask her about the vaccine... And contraception, too.

MOM

Okay, you tell Dad you're not going. For contraception, we'll go to mine, together. If Dad wanted you to see a gynecologist, why didn't he tell me?

MATHILDE

I think it was Sabine who wanted it most.

MOM

But come on! It's a mother's role to take her daughter to the gynecologist... It's a step no mother wants to miss. We'll go and see mine together.

February 2015. At the circus school

MILA

Mathilde, I wanted to talk to you about something...

MATHILDE

Yes ?

MILA

Wait, come on, we're getting away.

MATHILDE

What's going on?

MILA

In fact, I don't really want to talk about it around me, because I don't want everyone to feel sorry for me, I mean, we're not old enough to be sad about this kind of thing and I don't want others to try to console me or give me their opinion or whatever. But I wanted to talk to you about it, because I'm going through a bit the same situation as yours...

MATHILDE

What do you mean?

MILA

My mother met a woman. She says she still loves my father but doesn't know who to choose. My father has decided to divorce her.

MATHILDE

Ah, damn it! I'm sorry, I...

MILA

It's okay, don't worry, but I was wondering if you had any advice for this kind of, uh, situation.

MATHILDE

Well... For me, the most important thing is that everyone keeps talking to everyone else, that there's no breakdown in communication. You don't want you and your brother to become your parents' carrier pigeons. Because that's a real pain in the ass.

MILA

And as for my mother and her new girlfriend... Do you have any specific advice?

MATHILDE

So, no... I can give you advice on how to deal with your parents' divorce, but when it comes to having a lesbian mother... I've got nothing special to say. Except that it's *cool*, after all, it's a new life. Have you ever met your mother's girlfriend?

April 2015. In the car

MOM

Can I drop you at dad's now?

MATHILDE

Yes... hopefully they won't be here when I arrive.

MOM

Why do you say that?

MATHILDE

It's nothing special. It's just that... lately, I don't feel like going to 19.

MOM

Why?

MATHILDE

I don't feel very comfortable there. I have the impression that Dad absolutely wants us to be a perfect little traditional family: Mum, Dad and their children. But we're not a perfect little family, we could never be. We're a blended family, and that's just fine... Over there, I feel that everything is artificial. He's even invented a way of saying hello to each other: we all have to gather in a circle and shout "Biiii... bisous!", as if it were a war cry.

MOM

Oh yeah, still... I didn't know.

MATHILDE

And that's not all. Dad has also invented a national family holiday. He wants us to get together every July 20 to celebrate the anniversary of our first date with Sabine. When I was little, I thought it was funny. In the last year or two, I've realized it's weird. I'd like to play along, to please Dad and all that, but I can't anymore. Now I think it just sounds wrong.

MOM

You know, Dad always had these weird obsessions... Back when we were married, he was always showing you maps of the Alps. And the bread... The bread had to be perfect. Especially at *weekends*! On *weekends,* he wanted to eat the best bread possible. He had his own criteria: a shiny crust, a crumb that wasn't overcooked... On Sunday mornings, he'd get in the car and drive an hour to his favorite bakery in some godforsaken village. As for the perfect little family... I think Dad's parents really wanted their four sons to each start a nice, normal family. To make matters worse, Papi always made his four sons compete with each other...

99

MATHILDE

... and her grandchildren too! We couldn't draw together without it turning into a drawing contest...

MOM

... and by the time we were all old enough to have children, and none of us had any yet, Grandpa was always blaming us. To encourage us to have them, he finally said he'd leave all his books to the first grandchild born. In the end, Dad was the only one of the four sons to have the perfect little family Grandpa expected, until the divorce. And then it all fell apart!

MATHILDE

Maybe that's why Grandma and Grandpa didn't want to talk to you after the divorce. Not so much out of homophobia, but rather because they were disappointed to see the most perfect little family their sons had ever founded implode, and that Dad would like to be able to put back together again.

Christmas 2016. In Figeac

Johann and Mamie look at the photos in the 2017 calendar. In April, four photos line up. Gisèle, Christine, Nathalie and Sabine. Our three aunts and our mother-in-law. The montage is subtitled "Hommage aux mères de famille".

JOHANN

Oh, how cute, all the moms!

MAMIE

Right?

Stunned by Johann's remark, I look at my brother, my grandmother, then at the photos of the four women. All six are smiling.

Johann and my grandmother turn the calendar page together. The paper doesn't even squeak against the iron spiral.

It's unreal. Neither my brother nor my grandmother notice Mom's absence from the ranks of mothers. In the living room, I can hear the sound of wrapping paper being torn, and Émile's voice singing "Il est né le divin enfant" ("The divine child is born"). Perfect harmony. For a moment, I feel far away from the others and their reunion, and I understand the implicit meaning behind Johann's remark. In my paternal family, the consensus is that my mother doesn't exist. We don't talk about her.

Gisèle, Christine, Nathalie, Sabine are "mothers of families". But "maman Marieke" doesn't deserve the tribute my grandfather pays to the others. For, although she is a mother, she no longer has a family in which to play the role of mother.

At my paternal grandparents', I have to pretend that my father, his wife and children are my only family. Yet Isabelle is no less familiar to me than Sabine. Is my family divided into two parts? Do I have two separate families? Are Johann and Zoé my only real family? None of these hypotheses seem right to me. It's the word "family" that doesn't fit. I don't have a family: I'm surrounded by familiar people.

April 2017. On the beach in Perpignan

MATHILDE

Say, Mom, do you own anything from 31?

MOM

No, nothing at all. This house belonged to Isabelle's father. When he died, he left it to his wife. When she dies in turn, the house will go to Isabelle.

MATHILDE

What about you?

MOM

Savings, and half the apartment in Perpignan.

MATHILDE

Isabelle has the other half?

MOM

Yes.

MATHILDE

What if one of you dies?

MOM

You won't be able to share it until we're both dead. That's why Isabelle and I made a pact. We wanted to protect each other's children in the event of death.

MATHILDE

Why should we? None of us is very mean. I don't think Johann, Zoé or I would kick Isabelle out of Perpignan if you died, or that Quentin and Éli would chase you out if you did.

MOM

You never know.

MATHILDE

And why did you decide to live in Isabelle's mother's house? It would have been so much easier if we'd moved into a new house! In that case, Quentin and Éli saw our arrival as an invasion, and we, on the other hand, didn't really fit in at 31.

MOM

Isabelle and I thought about it. It was what we wanted to do at first, but it was too complicated and too expensive. At the time, I didn't have a job. I only gave private lessons and English classes at the Saint-Louis school. My salary was minuscule. We couldn't rent or buy another house. In our situation, we couldn't refuse a free roof under which we could live with our five children without being too cramped.

MATHILDE

Well, the house thing wasn't that bad. The worst part was the secrets.

MOM

Sometimes we think we have to lie to protect ourselves.

MATHILDE

You asked us to lie to others, and you lied to us too. For example, when you told us you met at the gym, right?

MOM

Yes, we met because you and Quentin had become friends in first grade. We didn't know each other until we took you to play at each other's houses.

MATHILDE

I knew it!

MOM

We told you that so you wouldn't feel guilty. Maybe it was a mistake. In the beginning, we made a lot of mistakes. We didn't know any more than you do about how a blended family works. In the end, I don't think we did too badly. I'm glad everyone came through without too many scars.

June 2017. Apartment B36 in the Langevin student residence, Lyon

It's vacation time already. Diane has invited five childhood friends to share the apartment. The apartment isn't very big: with ten people, it's a tight squeeze. But the guests are only staying for four days. The other roommates and I agreed to let Diane host them.

I enter our apartment. When I turn on the door to hold it open, I'm startled. I stand still for a few seconds, my eyes wide with surprise at the closed door.

Last week, I had left a pot of multi-colored chalk in the common room, so that everyone could draw or write messages on the front door.

Diane's friends covered it with blue and pink inscriptions. They wrote conservative political slogans in capital letters. In the middle, four characters hold hands: a little boy and his father, both in blue, a mother in a pink triangle, and a little girl who is a scale model.

For a moment, I think I'm in the wrong apartment. I look around. No, I'm home. My dishes are drying by the sink, my posters adorn the walls, my bedroom is at the end of the hall.

I look at the front door again. The manifesto pour tous logo welcomes me, laughing, into my own interior. I punch the wall. I feel naked, dirty, ashamed of my home. Please, don't let anyone in, don't let anyone see this, don't let anyone think that I, myself…

I can hear the door chuckling. Guests must have laughed out loud as they wrote on it. The door now screams the memory of their giggles. I turn around. I reread. I step back. I scream. The white walls have fists to beat me with. I can't defend myself or counterattack.

I'm listening at Diane's bedroom door. They're out. No target for the revolt that growls, screams inside me to let it out. I listen at the other doors. The apartment is empty. There's no one to show the inscriptions to, denounce them to and condemn them before. No one to ask if I'm hallucinating.

I have rabies.

Rage at being mocked, violated, as if raped for defiling my home. Hateful worms swarm in my windpipe. As I put my hand to my throat, I can feel them squirming. Behind me, dishes continue to drip slowly over the sink. I tip them over, then kick the chairs. They topple over with a loud crash. The floor shakes with laughter. I hold on to the only chair that hasn't fallen over. In my thoughts, fragments of arguments denouncing the drawings emerge, hurried and confused. They jostle my mind, which becomes bogged down and enraged.

Too much anger to verbalize. I sit down.

With my head in my hands, I feel the vibrations of rage hitting my abdomen on my forehead. Words fall apart. There's nothing left to say but screams. I bang my fist against the table, and cry with my head in my hands.

I stay like this for a long time. I listen to the return of calm. Gently, the walls pick up the cutlery I've scattered, then retract their fists. With a final jolt, the floor raises the chairs. Soon I can't hear the door chuckle.

July 2018. In the car

Mom

It's true that I took care of you more than Dad did. Since I wasn't working, you kids were my whole life... In fact, one of the hardest things for me to do after the divorce was to eat. Because my role as a mother was to feed my children. I couldn't imagine anyone else doing it... I was panicked at the idea of leaving you with Dad for almost a whole week. He'd never cooked a day in his life!

Mathilde

Ah, yes, sometimes he made mashed potatoes.

Mom

Really?

MATHILDE

Yes, he was proud of his super-sticky mashed potatoes. We called it dad-mash...

August 2018. In Figeac

MAMIE

... and with the old photos, there was this notebook... When you were little, I used to write down the funny and surprising things that children sometimes say, you know... Here, for example:

> Zoé wakes up from her nap. I go to her room to fetch her. We descend the stairs. She pushes aside the strands of hair that fall across her forehead, saying:
> - Oh dear! I can't see my eyes...

MATHILDE

Cute.

MAMIE

And another, this time from Johann... It's from when you weren't born yet. Listen to this:

> Paul, Marieke and Johann arrive by car in Figeac. Johann gets out of the car and says:
> - When I grow up, I'm going to move to the front and have two dads!

MATHILDE

Ah.

MAMIE

Haha! And wait until I find something funny you've told us...

MATHILDE

Well, Timothée's parents' house is beautiful!

JOHANN

Yeah, it's a rich house!

MATHILDE

It's a good match.

JOHANN, *to Zoé*

Admit it, that's why you're dating him.

ZOÉ

Nonsense! Instead of talking nonsense, Johann, what's going on in your life right now?

MATHILDE

Is that true? Did you meet any girls in the U.S.?

JOHANN

Well, that's just it... I wanted to take advantage of not being with Dad and Sabine to tell you... Something happened, but not with a girl... with a boy.

MATHILDE

Oh!

ZOÉ

Tell me, tell me!

JOHANN

Well... His name's Teddy, and he was a camp counselor, like me... We met on the second or third day because we were organizing an activity together for the kids. After that, we kept bumping into each other. So, over the summer, we talked a lot. But, in August, we both had a lot of work to do, and we never had the same groups of children to look after, so we didn't see each other too much. And then, in the last week, as the end of the camp approached, we arranged to meet up in the evening. At first, it was just to chat; and then, on the penultimate evening, we went to the other side of the lake, to a corner of the banks which is superbly beautiful. And it was perfect... There was a magnificent sunset in front of us, with the lake, the mountains, everything... And then we kissed...

ZOÉ

It's so romantic!

MATHILDE

But did you know you liked boys?

JOHANN

Well, no. Teddy was surprised too. He asked me, "Aren't you straight?" I told him, "Yes, I'm pretty *straight*."

ZOÉ

What does it mean?

JOHANN

That you like people of the opposite sex. But Teddy, I thought he was so handsome that I didn't care if he was a boy. He has very, very beautiful eyes. I think, actually, that's what matters to me. Not the sex, the eyes.

MATHILDE

Do you now consider yourself bi?

JOHANN

More pansexual, I think.

ZOÉ

Translation?

JOHANN

That means I can like anybody. Straight, gay, dude, chick, trans, bi, intersex, non-binary... it doesn't matter. As long as the person has beautiful eyes.

Mathilde

And you're going to tell the old folks?

Johann

To Mom and Isabelle, yes, I'll tell them.

Zoé

They're going to be so happy.

Mathilde

What about Dad and Sabine?

Johann

I don't think so... If it had been serious, maybe. Right now, it's just a vacation... I'll probably never see Teddy again. So, no, I won't say anything. You don't have to.

October 2019. On the 19th

Two series of photos are displayed in the entrance hall.

On the first are three portraits: of Zoé, Johann and me, aged between five and ten. My grandfather captioned the photos according to our attitudes. Zoé is "the rascal", Johann "the thinker" and I'm "the teacher".

The second series of photos also features three portraits in a row: Émile, Samuel and Marguerite, our little brothers and sister. The photos, in the same format as ours, are captioned "the rascal", "the thinker" and "the clown".

Mathilde, to Dad

Why does Grandpa always put old photos of the three of us together with those of the little ones?

Dad

Why do you ask?

Mathilde

I don't like it.

Dad

What's bothering you?

Mathilde

It gives me the impression that they're confusing us. In their eyes, Émile, Samuel and Marguerite are miniature reproductions of Johann, Zoé and me. As if we were all the same. Even though we don't have the same history, nor the same family. It's as if they want to erase your past with Mom, and pretend that Johann, Zoé and I are Sabine's children too...

Dad

What are you talking about?

Mathilde

Here, everyone wants to look like a clean-cut family. That's why we erase Mom. The kids don't even know who she is!

Dad

That's not true! We're talking to the kids about your mom. Here's an example! Before the vacations, Émile seemed very anxious. He kept telling me: "You have two lovers. Normally, we shouldn't have two lovers! I couldn't understand it, it pissed me off. One day I asked him who my second lover was. He said, "It's Mum Marieke, because you live with Mum and Mum Marieke. So I explained to him that I'd been very much in love with Marieke, that I'd even had children with her, but that now it was over and I only loved his mommy. And we made a family tree together, with everyone, even your mom, Mathilde. It made him feel better. He stopped throwing tantrums over something, and went back to the way he was before. He's back to his old self, so he can see who Mama Marieke is.

Mathilde

Yes, but before you explained who it was, he thought you were still with her, so it's good that it was all a blur to him. Because you weren't telling him enough.

Dad

Well, yes... That's right... Sabine and I thought that one day we'd explain it to Samuel and Marguerite too, so they wouldn't be lost like Émile. For the moment, they're too small.

Mathilde

I don't think you have to be a grown-up to understand that.

Dad

You know, this isn't a very usual situation.

Mathilde

So what? Children can understand unusual situations better than some adults.

*

Émile's family tree looks realistic. The trunk and roots are smeared brown, while the branches are light green. At the very top of the A4 sheet, cursive handwriting hangs the names of the six children at the top of the tree: Johann, Mathilde, Zoé, Émile, Samuel and Marguerite.

At the other end of the drawing, four roots represent my little brother's grandparents. In the middle, on the trunk, Paul and Sabine's first names are linked in blue felt-tip pen. On the left, Émile has written his mother's name. However, there is no line to link Marieke to another name.

Isabelle is not in the picture.

- Yes, it was nice to hear from you too, but, uh, wait... I wanted to ask you something... Do you still have a little time?

- ...

- Great, thanks. Actually, I need your advice... I wanted to ask you... Am I allowed to be bi?

- ...

- Of course, but I'm asking you this because Isabelle says all the time that we necessarily prefer girls *or* boys, and it's eating away at me... Because I know I like both. But, because she keeps saying that, I've come to wonder whether I really like boys *and* girls, or whether I only like girls, and that, because of the prevailing heterosexuality, I force myself to believe that I like boys too.

- ...

- Well... basically, this summer, when I was staying with you, there was a meal where we were talking about Johann... And Isabelle said something like: "Anyway, I was sure he was gay, you could tell, he never talked to us about girls, the girls always had too much hair or too many breasts to please him, and then he was always talking about his boyfriend Julien..." Except that Johann isn't gay, he's pansexual. So I say this to Isabelle, and she replies: "I don't believe in bisexuality. Sex is like food: you can like two different dishes, but there's bound to be one you prefer." I said no, because I know I like girls and boys, and I don't prefer either one. At least, I don't think I do. I don't know if she listened to me, because then she replied that she was sure that, in ten years' time, I'd be coming home with a girl.

- ...

- Okay, except that two days later, I'm talking about our plans to set up a training space with Mikhail, and she says to me: "Ah!

I wouldn't advise you to buy something for two now, imagine that, in two years' time, you realize you're a lesbian..." But, shit, just because that's what happened to you doesn't mean it's going to happen to me too!

- ...

- Maybe, but this sex thing, which is like food, dogged me for two or three weeks, and I kept asking myself whether or not I was wrong about my sexual orientation. As a result, I've been unable to enjoy being with Mikhail... And it's not like it's anything new. Isabelle has been implying for years that I'm a lesbian, and since you and Dad divorced, I've been wondering...

- ...

- Well, yes, I've already tried it with a girl. With two girls at the same time, in fact. A long time ago, I was fourteen or fifteen. Fifteen, I think.

- ...

- Yes, it was good.

- ...

- No, it's true... In fact, when you asked me if I'd ever had sex with girls, I'd say no, because for me, at the time, "sexual experience" meant penetration. So I didn't consider what I'd experienced to be a sexual experience. And I didn't want to talk about it, because I knew Isabelle would take it as proof that I was a lesbian, and that she'd be too pleased with herself... I could already hear her repeating: "I told you, Mathilde, that you're a lesbian! Even though, at the time, I was also sleeping with a boy... Anyway, just to avoid giving Isabelle the pleasure of believing she was right, which she wasn't, I didn't want to tell you.

- ...

- Yes, I enjoy it with Mikhail. That's why I ask myself questions, because I also like sex with boys...

- ...

- I know... but... it's also that... what can I say...

- ...

- Well... I don't want to be the conventional one in the family. You and Isabelle dared to leave your husbands and your well-ordered lives to live your love story. Quentin and Johann are having affairs with boys. I realized that I was jealous of Johann, because now you and he have something more in common...

- ...

- Yes, it's true that being bi isn't conventional either... I'm not sure why I'm telling you this. So you think I have the right to like boys *and* girls?

- ...

- I'm in. Hey, Mom... One more thing...

- ...

- Do you still love me, even if I'm not quite like you?

- ...

- I know, I know... I just wanted to check.

- ...

- ...

- ...

- Thank you.

8.
Interview with Jeanne, 18, and Martin, 11

What do you know about your design?

JEANNE: My father set aside some seeds, which were put into my mother's body, our mother's body. It was all done by hand.

Do you still see your father?

MARTIN: Yes, he comes some *weekends.*

JEANNE: The rest of the time, we live mainly with our two moms. My father didn't want to have children, but when my two mothers asked him if he'd be willing to be the father, he agreed. We can go to his house whenever we want and he's free, and he has a room in the house: it's pretty flexible.

To what extent do you consider him your father?

JEANNE: I don't know, I don't really know the definition of a father... We call him "Dad".

MARTIN: He's our father.

JEANNE: It's a family format that's a bit different...

Do you consider yourself to have three parents?

JEANNE: Yes, we have three parents, two moms and a dad, whom we consider in the same way.

Are your mothers married?

JEANNE: They're just civil partners. Sophie, our biological mother, carried both of us. We have the same genes. Legally, however, Laurence has no rights over us, since our father recognized us. Under current French law, there's no room for a third parent. When we're both eighteen, Laurence will be able to adopt us. I've just turned eighteen, but we're waiting for Martin to do the same. We'll kill two birds with one stone!

Can you tell me about your upbringing?
JEANNE: Well, we don't have anything special to say. Our parents follow us. There's no difference with heteroparental families.

Do you talk about your family with your classmates?
MARTIN: At my school, all my friends know that I have two mothers.
JEANNE: It was the same for me, even if I'm perhaps more of a protestor than Martin. As soon as the subject came up in class, I was always there to witness the reactions and say, "You can see I'm normal! That said, there's a real difference between middle school and high school. We're in a small town and, in middle school, people were a bit more astonished, whereas in high school, they're more in the mode: "Wow, so *cool!*"
MARTIN: On the other hand, none of my teachers know anything about it. I asked her for help because I'd forgotten to tell my parents that there was no canteen.

How did she take the news about your moms?
MARTIN: Good.

(Sophie, one of Jeanne and Martin's mothers, arrives and joins the conversation).

Which of your mothers went to "parent-teacher meetings"? Were any of the teachers surprised?

SOPHIE: The gym teacher knows all about it. I'm a teacher, so I've had her daughters. Otherwise, we've always had a great welcome. Except for Jeanne's enrolment in the preparatory class: I went with Laurence. The principal paused for a moment, which wasn't very pleasant, but that was the surprise! Still, Laurence didn't take it well: it hit her where it hurt, since she had no rights over the children.

JEANNE: Maybe it's luck, but we've never had any inappropriate remarks, even from teachers.

Jeanne, do you consider yourself an activist or a committed person?

JEANNE: Martin and I were dragged to the demonstrations, so we got involved. I have friends who come from quite religious families, Muslim or even Christian, so it's interesting to have discussions with them: I have a friend who's Muslim, and you feel that it's blocking... So I like talking about it. I did it more in high school; in college, I did it less, I just explained my case and didn't necessarily get into debates.

MARTIN: At first, I'm a bit afraid to say *it,* but it doesn't matter, because if someone asks me a question, I answer that my mothers are gay and that I have a father.

JEANNE: I'm the kind of person who asks people questions: it brings up the subject, and I see if I can be their friend or not.

And what do you say when people ask you the same question?

JEANNE: I say, "I have two moms and one dad, and both my moms are together. Afterwards, people usually ask me how I was born. People imagine that my father and my biological mother were together, then they split up and my mother got involved with a girl. So I explain that it's not the right scenario...

Jeanne, you said you sometimes probed the field, in the beginning, to find out whether the person you were talking to was suitable or not. What criteria do you have to meet when it comes to these questions?

JEANNE: You shouldn't be homophobic. Afterwards, some of my friends ask questions because of their upbringing. I try to open up new horizons for them. I'll just put it here, and then we'll see tomorrow...

And at home, Martin, have you experienced any debates? Has the issue of PMA, for example, been discussed in class or with friends?

JEANNE *(to Martin)*: Do you know what PMA is? It's medically assisted procreation.

SOPHIE: We managed to make you with a father, but in other countries, it's different, and it wasn't authorized in France. And now it's being voted on, so there's been a lot of talk about it, but it wasn't discussed at school.

JEANNE: I saw a lot of it on social networks... In high school, I talked about it with my friends, but not with my teachers.

What was your experience of the upheavals surrounding "marriage for all"?

SOPHIE: It was 2012-2013. *(To Jeanne:)* You were eleven when you entered the sixth grade... We were received at the ministry with the APGL.

JEANNE: So we did this event, and we used to go to the demonstrations in Nantes, since we live nearby. One thing struck me: a group of guys were passing by, masks over their mouths... I mean, they were against this law. It struck me.

SOPHIE: With you two, there was Paris and Nantes: we took you twice.

JEANNE: Didn't we make more?

SOPHIE: I remember one demonstration under the water and another with the homophobes... It was great!

You mentioned the APGL. Did you spend much time with this association? For example, did you take part in "Lily of the Valley weekends", etc.?

Sophie: No, not "Lily of the Valley weekends", but yurt weekends in the region, yes! We always go, and we offer our big house for hosting. As it happens, we haven't hosted for a year, but we've always done it so that our children can meet others. We have friends because of it, even if we don't go there as much. There were some nice people there!

Jeanne and Martin, do you feel that you belong to a community, or that you have something special that sets you apart from others in a positive way?

JEANNE: A feeling of belonging to a community, yes. I'd like to go into law when I'm older, and specifically into the law on same-sex families, because that's where I've been and because I think it's a positive thing, because it opens the door to things other than a heteroparental family. Even if I don't feel like I stand out from the crowd, I find it really beneficial.

MARTIN: It's unique.

Does this give you a more open view of what a family is?

JEANNE: We know that many different families exist. I think it's interesting!

Do you feel discriminated against? For example, once you've told no one that you have two mothers and a father, do you see a change in attitude?

JEANNE: I've never experienced that. I have to say that, in general, people get to know me a little before I tell them anything. They see that it's irrelevant.

You have three families, on your parents' side, three pairs of grandparents. Do your biological mother's grandparents consider you more like their grandchildren than your social mother's family?

JEANNE: No, it's the same thing.

SOPHIE: Even Laurence's parents are worried about the inheritance. They know that Jeanne and Martin won't receive the same thing: they've talked to Laurence about it. Nico's parents are deceased, but they considered Martin and Jeanne to be grandchildren like any others.

JEANNE: Yes, we used to eat at their place on Sundays.

Within families, the subject of homoparenting is sometimes taboo. Have you also felt this way?

SOPHIE: It was complicated at first, because we didn't have the children. But having children legitimized us as parents and as a family. Today, my mother calls Laurence her second daughter. Children give us a place. Without them, it might have taken longer. Nevertheless, our parents have come a long way. They've been adorable.

Jeanne and Martin, in which social class do you think you'll evolve?

JEANNE: Modest, but we're fine. Our parents have stable jobs, we've never lacked for anything, we're lucky enough to be able to go on vacation...

Jeanne, you mentioned earlier that some of our comrades come from very religious backgrounds. Is this also the case for you?

JEANNE: Our grandparents were a bit Christian, but not very much; they went to mass from time to time...

SOPHIE: I used to go to mass every Sunday when I was little, but my parents eventually gave up. That's why I say my parents went through a lot of changes! There are, in my generation, other parents whose children are homosexual, for whom it's more complicated, who have thrown them out... Unfortunately, I think this is still the case, in certain circles; it's not a question of generation, it's really a question of mentality.

SOPHIE *(to Martin)*: Would you have preferred to be in a family with a mom and dad?

MARTIN : No!

SOPHIE: When he was a little boy, Martin came home from nursery school in the petite or moyenne section, and he said to Laurence with a look of catastrophy for the others: "But Malau, the others don't have a Malau!" He imagined that all children had two moms and a dad, and he thought that was great: he was sad for those who only had one mom and one dad! We thought it was cute, but also thought: "What's he going to say when he realizes that it's not like that for the others?"

8. Interview with Jeanne, 18, and Martin, 11

How do you see the future of homoparentality and homoparental families in France?

JEANNE: We're making progress, but there's still a long way to go, as shown by the debates on PMA.

SOPHIE *(to Martin)*: Do you think the future will be more favorable to homosexuals? Will they be more accepted?

MARTIN: I think we're on the right track, I think there's hope.

9.
Laura, aged 31

My name is Laura, I'm 31 and I have two mothers.

My little "half-sister" is called Louise, and I love her with a love that couldn't be fuller. I will always be shocked by the formula that reduces our bond to a "half-bond", because we come from different parents.

Louise and I are ten years apart, a decade that I feel is important to underline in view of the evolution of people's views on the position of the child within a lesbian couple. Unlike my little sister, who was conceived by artificial insemination with an anonymous donor in Belgium, I was born of a physical relationship between a man and my mother.

One evening in 1987, my mother, who was living with a woman at the time, went to a seminar in Berlin as part of her work for the public hospital service. There she met a medical equipment company director. They become close friends. I would show the tip of my nose nine months later. To this day, my father wonders if it was all calculated, if my mother simply wanted a child or if there was indeed a carnal bond between them. I don't know.

A few years later, it was by chance that they met again at a business meeting. My father remembers this moment and likes to tell me about it:

- Your mother hadn't changed. I was happy to see her again and *secretly* thought we'd end the night as we had then. We exchanged a few words, and she soon showed me a photo of you, implying that you were my daughter.

*

I must have been two or three years old when Mamou came into my life. Unlike my sister, I didn't come from a joint project between the two of them, but from a project linked solely to my mother. It's obvious that this difference played a part in the relationship difficulties I had with my second mother. The nickname "Mamou" didn't appear until I was 10, when my sister was born.

I remember being very hard on Mamou, mainly as a teenager. I recently found some writings I had written. In them, I expressed my anger, sadness and sense of injustice towards this different family. On the *other hand,* I had a very close relationship with my mother.

When I was in elementary school, I remember my mother telling me not to tell my friends that I had two moms, certainly thinking she was protecting me. She reassured me that it wasn't a question of lying, just of "not telling".

When a classmate asked me:

- Who's the lady with the short hair who picks you up at night?

I replied

- She's my aunt.

I also remember the first birthdays at home, when my friends would realize that "my aunt" was living with me, that she didn't have her own room, that photos of her and my mother were hanging on the walls, and so on. I can still see myself giving them a lot of nonsensical explanations to keep them from finding out the truth.

My mother thought she was doing the right thing by trying to protect me from childish mockery. I was afraid of betraying her by saying the wrong thing. So I hid the truth and gradually realized that, in the school environment, the approach to homoparentality was totally different between my sister and me. Indeed, while I was creating a salt dough sculpture for the birthday of the dad I didn't have, ten years later, the system adapted to allow my little sister, Louise, to create a beautiful pearl necklace for the "Fête des mamous".

Unlike me, Louise always spoke openly about our parents' homosexuality. I spent my early school years lying. From a very early age, we're taught that when a person lies, it's to avoid saying something bad. In my opinion, a child who is asked to knowingly lie, for whatever reason, will unconsciously deduce that what he or she is hiding is bad. What's more, if the person asking him to lie is a parent, he'll be afraid of betraying him and no longer being loved. So I think the main reason I've had difficulty accepting my mothers' homosexuality is because I've been asked to hide it.

As for my father, my mother explained that she didn't want him to interfere in my upbringing, but that if he wanted to, he could see me from time to time. Even though he was married with two children, he decided to get to know me, while making sure that none of his family got wind of my existence. I can't remember exactly when we started seeing each other, but I do know that when he picked me up outside school, I was proud. With my childlike eyes, I was happy when he picked me up in his beautiful car. I used to tell my "school friends" that my parents were separated and that I lived with my mother.

However, our relationship hasn't always been easy. During my adolescence, we went through a period of disconnection. I must have been 13 when, one day, I joined my father to spend some time with him. We exchanged a few words. As usual, he gave me some money... except that, this time, my blood ran cold. Somewhere between sadness and anger, I threw his bills in his face and shouted:

- Who do you think I am? You'll never buy me! You can't make up for lost time like that!

I was in pain, convinced I'd been abandoned, angry at being a hidden child, and sad at feeling I'd been bought. After a lot of personal work, I now understand that this was not her goal, and above all that the abandonment never existed. I realize that the money was his way of being present and pleasing me. We often talk about that moment, which was very painful for both of us...

Today, I have a close relationship with the man I sometimes allow myself to call my father. We've finally come to terms with each other. He gained confidence in me and in my ability not to betray him to his family; I understood that I had to accept this somewhat atypical position in order to solidify our relationship. The peculiarity of our mixed history, our strong characters and our hypersensitivity sometimes lead us to have heated exchanges; nevertheless, each of us wants to preserve our strong yet fragile bond. In short, to this day, my father is part of my life; nevertheless, I'll never consider him one of my parents.

*

Very sociable by nature, I had a lot of friends when I became a teenager, but even the closest ones didn't know that I had two moms. Then, as time went by and my self-confidence grew, I gradually managed to open up about it. After dating only boys, I had my first homosexual experience when I was seventeen.

Contrary to what many people think, having a lesbian mother doesn't necessarily make things easier when it comes to acceptance. For my part, I remember like it was yesterday the first discussion I had with my mother on this subject. At home, we rarely broached the subject of "boyfriends". Things were understood naturally; my moms knew about my adventures and let me live my experiences as long as they seemed healthy to them. That day, however, my mother sat by my bed and warned me about the difficulties that could arise from what she called "a lifestyle choice". I remember listening to her carefully as she told me that my hypersensitivity would not help me on this path and that, given the choice, it was preferable for me to opt for a simpler life. In other words, heterosexuality. Today, I understand that my mother wanted to protect me from malevolent people who might have crossed my path. Or was the very idea that I might suffer because of my sexual orientation unbearable for her?

As the daughter of a lesbian couple, I have suffered from the social belief that growing up *gay* increases the risk of becoming gay. I feel I have to keep explaining that my homosexuality has nothing to do with my parents' lifestyle. On the other hand, I'd like to thank my moms because, without them, I'd never have had the courage to assume my preferences. Perhaps, like many others who weren't so lucky, I would have chosen to be unhappy rather than assume my homosexuality.

I insist: contrary to popular belief, growing up in a homoparental environment does not increase the "risk" of a child becoming homosexual. In fact, becoming homosexual is not a choice. The only choice we make is whether or not to accept this difference. Conversely, I think our parents' lifestyle enabled my sister and me to develop an open mind at a very early age. Difference leads to tolerance and, *de facto,* a broader view of the world and the many paths it offers.

The same applies to religion. Our mothers have always given us the opportunity to make our own choices, while providing us with the elements we need to understand. We've been lucky enough to

9. Laura, aged 31

grow up with parents who don't share the same beliefs. My mother is an atheist. Mamou had a Catholic upbringing, surrounded by religious parents. She instilled her way of thinking in us without forcing us to adhere to it. I've never been a believer; my sister wanted to be baptized. Today, we're both atheists, although we sometimes go to church on December 24 to please our grandfather. Thanks to this diversity of convictions, I feel that my sister and I have been able to choose our path and live in harmony with who we are.

*

Today, I accept my homosexuality and that of my mothers. However, for a long time, I kept a very modest side to myself, possibly linked to my history. A sort of embarrassment about "showing off" with another woman. As my love life progressed, and thanks in particular to certain women who shared my life, I learned not to dwell on the way others looked at me, while often continuing to conceal, at least initially, my mothers' homosexuality. In the professional sphere, for example, I never say a word about it.

More generally, I feel I spend a lot of energy being wary of human stupidity. My family is my treasure. I will do everything in my power to take care of it. I no longer have the strength to dwell on the judgment of intolerant people. Maybe things will change in time, but right now I'd rather avoid having to prove that I'm not mentally unbalanced. Of course, fighting is my comfort zone, because "the best defense is a good offense". However, I'm trying to develop other ways of being, as this way of operating is exhausting and far from always constructive.

*

In conclusion, in my opinion, growing up as a child in a lesbian household is no more difficult than growing up in a family based on another model. Every child grows up in his or her own way; every teenager has his or her own experiences; every adult has things to sort out with himself or herself; no matter what parental example he or she receives. There are no more obstacles to living a happy life when you have two moms than when you have one mom and one dad, even if these obstacles can sometimes be of a different nature. I'd go even further: to be brought up in an unconventional family model is to be made more deeply aware of the values of tolerance.

Mamou used to say to me: "As many children as there are educations", and she was right. The problem is not the parental example we discover, but the educational model and the quality of the love we receive.

Since then, I've been projecting the idea of building a family. Having children is an option open to me. Being homosexual is not an obstacle. My mothers loved me and love me unconditionally. I'm proud to have had an upbringing full of beautiful values that I hope to pass on to my future children.

10.
Interview with Zoé, 18

Can you introduce yourself in a few words?

My name is Zoé, I'm eighteen and I'm in my second year of law at Lille University. I also work as a supervisor in a secondary school.

What do you know about how you were conceived?

I was conceived by MAP in Belgium in 2001. My sister and I were conceived in the same way. We were lucky enough to have the same donor, even though we don't have the same mother - it's funny, but in the end, it doesn't really matter.

Are your mothers married or living together?

Both of them! They were civil partners, then married. They became civil partners in 2002, then married in 2013, as soon as the law was passed. They were looking forward to it so they could adopt each other's children.

What are your mothers' professions?

Françoise is a researcher at the CNRS, specializing in the combustion of flames; Géraldine is a project manager in a popular education association.

How were you perceived as a rainbow child?

I was lucky. Even in college, I never felt any different about it. Of course, I knew who to tell and who not to tell, but that didn't stop me from getting on well with people I didn't tell!

How did you decide who to tell about your situation?

It could be religious... or not! Sometimes, it was just people talking backwards: in those cases, I didn't even take the time to tell them because I knew it wasn't worth it.

How do you react today when you see that, for many people, a family is "a father and a mother"?

I'm not offended by them. I feel rather sorry for them, because I find them ridiculous. Luckily, in my life, I don't meet people like that, so they don't get to me.

Did you talk to your teachers about your family situation?

Up until secondary school, I went to small schools, so my teachers were all aware of it. I never got any nasty comments about it. My high school was huge, so the teachers didn't really know. When I had problems with certain teachers and they had to meet the parents, they were well aware that I had two mothers, but in terms of my schooling or the administration, I never had any problems at that level.

Did you meet any other rainbow children during your childhood?

Yes, because my moms are friends with gay couples who also have children. But, as far as I know, not in the school context.

Have you ever wanted to have children?

I've often imagined myself without children, but more and more as I get older, I find myself imagining having children in the future.

If you had someone from La Manif Pour Tous in front of you, what would you say?

First of all, if it's someone who doesn't know I come from a gay family, I'd say to them: "Does the way I'm behaving, physically, give you the impression that I'm lacking something? Do you feel that I've evolved differently from a normal child? Compared to the person right next to me, do you get the impression that we're different, that I'm weird or anything?" If she says no, I'll say, "You can see that your judgment is based on nonsense, because I come from a gay family!"

What if the person says, "Yes, you're weird"?

I'll ask him why, and we'll discuss it. But if the person is completely stubborn, I'm not going to waste my time with them!

What do you think of your donor?

My idea of him is: he's a giver. If I'm asked to meet him, I'll say yes, even though I don't miss him. How could I miss someone who was never part of my life?

Did growing up in a lesboparental environment lead you to develop specific representations of sexuality and gender identity?

It's a bit difficult to answer this question, because I don't know what I would have been like if I hadn't had two mothers. Having lived in a very open-minded family, I thought I had learned things that I might not have learned in another family... but I have friends with heterosexual parents who think like me.

Did your mothers talk to you about sexuality?

Yes, by saying to myself: "There's this and that, you can be this or that, there are lots of things out there". It wouldn't necessarily have been very different in another open-minded family. Since I was little, I've only been attracted to boys, so I assume I'm heterosexual. Nevertheless, I'm of the opinion that you don't fall in love with one sex.

Are you politically involved in the parenthood issues that concern you?

When I hear about *it, I* hear about *myself.* That's why I've taken part in certain demonstrations. However, I'm not committed to the point of fighting. If someone comes to talk to me about it, I answer and explain my point of view, but I'm not into constant struggle or commitment.

What's your general political leaning?

I'm quite sensitive to the politics of my country and, because of my studies, I'm also a bit forced into it. I'm interested in how it works and I'm gradually forming an opinion that's closer to left-wing ideas.

And your mothers?

They are rather left-wing atheists.

What is your opinion on the evolution of the recognition of new types of filiation?

Progress has been made. Even PMA has finally been passed - hallelujah! But when you realize that, in Belgium, the provisions that apply in France have been in place for a whole bunch of years, you have to ask yourself: why are there countries that are so much more advanced than us, even if some of them are even worse? Isn't it about time we got moving?

11.
Louise, 22 years old

My name is Louise, I'm 22 and I'm Laura's sister. Well, officially, her half-sister.

To give birth to me, my mothers chose to go to Belgium and use artificial insemination. So I was born of a donor whose identity I don't know, while Laura was born of a father she does know.

I've never suffered from not having a male presence in the family. I often use the word "father" to refer to my donor. My choice is not insignificant, as I distinguish "father" from "dad" and "parent". The donor is indeed my father, since I share half of my genes with him. From a scientific point of view, I am indeed his daughter. However, my real parents are my two mothers. Not having a blood relationship with my non-biological mother doesn't detract from the love I have for her and the strong bond that has developed between us.

The gift of my biological father was essential to my conception, but that doesn't mean I want to meet him. He hasn't and never will have the status of a parent to me, he wasn't present in my childhood, he wasn't involved in my education, he didn't support me as I progressed through life. Of course, he has always piqued my curiosity. I often wonder what he looks like, what prompted him to take on this gift, what he does for a living, what his character is like, and so on. Nevertheless, I've long since accepted that all these questions remain unanswered.

From the outset, my moms were honest with me about this father's place in our history, and why I wasn't allowed to know more about him. They also showed me that family values are less about blood ties than about the relationships forged within a household. I'm convinced that their openness and love helped me, beyond my questions, to accept my uniqueness.

*

When I think back, I'm impressed by the steps my mothers took to make my birth possible. It's quite a complex choice for a gay couple. All the more so as there are so many questions to be answered, including: who will carry the child? is insemination the best choice? where to go? how to raise the child without stigmatization? and so on... I'm also proud of the thought they must have put into making this decision. They were very united and strong on this issue. They took a lot of time to build up this project and reach the end of their desire. Having a child shouldn't require so many doubts and fears, but society doesn't make it easy for gay couples to take the necessary steps to experience the happiness of seeing their child grow up.

Despite, or perhaps because of, this adversity, we form a very close family. I'm not related by blood to my non-biological mom, but I've always considered her my second parent. She was as important to my upbringing as my biological mom, so for a long time I didn't pay much attention to the fact that, genetically, we're not related. I paid a little more attention to it when we learned more about genetics in SVT classes in secondary school, but it didn't affect my view of my family. I love my moms equally, and my sister is still my sister, not my half-sister. We grew up with the support of both our moms, so we share the same values; we have the same bond with our moms as "classic kids" have with their parents.

For me, blood ties have nothing to do with family, and vice versa. Family is a pillar on which we can rest if we falter; it supports us and helps us move forward in life. That's exactly how I feel about my parents and my sister. However, there were times when I wondered about the way my non-biological mother's family viewed me. My relationship with my grandparents was different from that with my cousins. I was jealous of them as a child! Since then, I've come to understand that the difference is linked to the greater geographical proximity between my cousins and my grandparents! I also have the impression that my grandparents didn't really know how to come up to me, how to show me that they considered me part of the family, perhaps a certain form of shyness towards me. But now I know that I mean as much to them as my cousins do.

When I grew up, I took a step back. I moved abroad. What a trigger! My grandparents and aunt opened up to me. The distance made our mutual affection tangible. I realized that I was just as important to them.

It helped me to accept the ups and downs of life. My mothers were separated for eight years. When they got back together, they were very quick to talk about marriage without mentioning it to us. It all happened very quickly. Marriage for all" had just been recognized, and they took the opportunity to make their return to married life official. It was a very simple occasion, involving family and close friends. The mayor of our village conducted the ceremony very well, she was very sympathetic and also very happy to attend this wedding between two women. Without question, I enjoyed this beautiful moment.

Later, other questions arose. Adoption, for example. My non-biological mother attached great importance to this. After marriage, this step was supposed to definitively seal her recognition as a parent. As for me, I know who my parents are, and I don't need any official paperwork to confirm it. However, from her point of view, by formalizing her importance in my sister's and my life, she would erase the frustration that her opinion didn't count towards authority, in official decision-making... So she chose to adopt Laura and me. I accepted her plan, which also showed how much she cared about us, and I supported her. But then disaster struck! The notary who was to ratify the adoption had not prepared the file at all. He seemed lost in the procedure, and we ended up leaving in a state of great frustration. For fear of being disappointed again, we didn't come back to the issue.

*

When children of lesbians testify, they sometimes talk about social rejection. As for me, I didn't suffer. I've always avoided lies, secrecy and secrets. Why hide the obvious? Why pretend? I prefer to accept my difference and move forward. Admittedly, my story is an original one; but, as a result, I've often wanted to tell others about it without pretence. It keeps me from beating around the bush; and it shows others that I feel just fine because I've received as much love and support from my moms as a heterosexual couple could have given me.

So, whenever the subject comes up, I talk about having two moms. I think it's a way for me to show that I'm proud of my parents, that I don't feel left out of society. It's my own little battle to open people's minds. I've always spoken openly about my parents' homosexuality. It helps to break down the misconceptions on the subject, the stereotypes that blind public opinion.

However, I don't want to take part in demonstrations or join associations. I want to devote my energy to other activities, and I don't want to force people to open their minds. I have nothing to prove to anyone. I only profess the obvious: love between two people of the same sex is just as beautiful and sincere as love between two people of the opposite sex. If people don't understand that, I've got nothing to do with them.

At school, my parents' homosexuality was pretty well accepted. In fact, I went to the same primary and secondary school as my sister. This may have made things easier, as almost all the teachers knew our story. Nevertheless, I spent half of my junior year in Mayotte, and from the third year through to the final year of high school, I went to schools where no one knew our family situation - without any worries either. Even at school, on those famous mother's or father's days when a child of lesbians feels the full force of her difference, the teachers have always been understanding.

More broadly, my experience suggests that the approach to homosexuality in schools is not class-dependent. I went from a middle-class elementary school, to an affluent middle school and then to a lower-class middle school. I didn't find that there were any big differences in the way people my age perceived us. I've always spoken openly about my two moms and, even in Mayotte where I rubbed shoulders with a lot of Muslims, I didn't feel any rejection. I like to think that, in general, homosexuality is accepted by my generation.

On the other hand, sometimes religion can play a role in acceptance. For example, I had the opportunity to speak with a Muslim friend. Whether in his country of origin, where Islam is king, or in

11. Louise, 22 years old

Hungary, where he now lives, he feels a profound disgust for homosexuals. The indoctrination he received as a child has affected him to such an extent that the presence of a homosexual inspires him with repulsion and obvious discomfort. Despite this, I've never heard him speak ill of homosexuals: he simply wants others to understand how he feels... and for everyone to go their own way. Strangely enough, he became good friends with a bisexual boy. As if, in some cases, people's view of homosexuality is rapidly changing, even in spite of themselves!

*

Being raised by two moms has not been without consequences for my own sexuality. Although I'd never been attracted to a girl until now, I began to question my preferences without taboos or barriers, earlier than my peers with heterosexual parents.

I've always considered love between two people of the same sex to be equal to love between two people of the opposite sex. As a child, I couldn't understand why some children didn't understand this, especially when they asked me a lot of questions about the bond between my two moms. Later, as I got older, I realized that many people weren't used to meeting same-sex couples. They also had trouble imagining how it was possible to feel an attraction for someone of the same sex. Of course, this preference can't be explained, but it's no different from heterosexual attraction! Homosexuality and heterosexuality work in the same way. Everyone should discover their preferences for themselves, without fear of being judged.

<h1 style="text-align:center">12.
Interview with Nathan, 16</h1>

How were you conceived?

I think it was in a Belgian clinic in Liège. I don't have much more information. I was conceived by PMA, with a donor.

Did your mothers ever tell you why they wanted to have children?

They just told me they wanted to have children like a normal couple. They did what they could. In fact, I have a little brother, two years my junior, who was conceived just like me.

Can you tell me about your family situation?

I have two mothers, who have been separated since I was seven. I have alternating custody: I go to one and the other every other week.

How do you feel about this separation?

When I was a child, I didn't take it very well, but I think it's the same for all children, whether they come from same-sex couples or not.

What do you think of your mothers' desire to have children?

Honestly, I understand the desire to have children, but the problem is that, in a same-sex family, the child has to assume the choice of parents; and it's not always easy to have two mothers.

What do you mean when you say you "take responsibility for your parents' choices"?

It's important not to let yourself be taken for a ride and not to fear the judgment of others.

For example, do you talk about situations you've experienced with your schoolmates?

With friends, it's often a bit strange when they first hear about it, but then, in general, it goes well, albeit always in a slightly different way.

How would you describe the situations in which you have to tell someone that you have two mothers? Does this happen at the beginning of a meeting, for example, or over time?

It usually happens when I get on well with someone, maybe after a year. I'm not going to tell them spontaneously. I never bring it up. That's the case with my girlfriend, for example.

Do you feel that having two mothers is an integral part of your identity?

It's something I can't deny, but it's not that important.

Do you think it's "normal" to have two mothers or to live with two mothers?

It depends on how you define normality. Let's say it's different.

What image and symbolism of the family do you draw from your experience?

It's mainly the image of the mother. I have two, I had... I don't know if I can say it like that... a very maternal childhood. Maybe we lacked a bit of paternal strength... In education, for example. I was always brought up with two women at home, never a father. I don't know if that was lacking in my upbringing, but it was different.

Did you notice any differences between your family situation and that of others, for example, when you were with friends who had both a mother and a father, or who lived in single-parent or blended families?

I don't pay much attention to it. In general, it's a bit more structured at home. Although… Maybe I have more freedom at home, but when I want to go out or do outside activities, it's more complicated, given that I've had more support in my life since kindergarten. I always find someone to help me at home.

How would you define this "maternal" dimension?

I was never abused as a child, unlike some of my friends. I was very rarely hit, unlike some of my friends. At home, there was always the father, who was the ultimate threat. They were afraid of being punished if they didn't do their homework, for example, whereas as far as I was concerned, I got a slap at worst, and that's as far as it went. I think the paternal side helps to frame the child, even if I'm not sure it's necessary. And by "maternal", I mean support: I was always listened to at home, I always felt good.

How does society view your family situation?

I haven't had any problems with this; in fact, the opposite is true: society does its utmost to integrate us into its citizenry, even if this doesn't come naturally to everyone.

So you would differentiate between the legal aspect and the more symbolic dimension of society, which would find it harder to accept your situation?

12. Interview with Nathan, 16

Yes. Society is a little less accepting but, in law, we are supported and helped as much as possible.

Do you think your mothers are discriminated against?
I don't think so. I know they both have jobs and things are going relatively well. One's a history-geography teacher, the other's an engineer. I think they're like me and they don't tell everyone, which avoids certain problems. In general, they're quite well received, and I haven't heard of any problems with them.

Do you know their political orientation? How do they relate to religion?
We don't talk politics, but I know they're rather left-wing. One of them is an atheist, and the other one is quite interested between several religions (it's not very clear to me).

Do you know why your mothers split up?
I'd say it's like a normal couple: there comes a point when things just don't work out, when they just don't get along. It has nothing to do with homoparenting.

Do you remember any particular events or things from the time they were together, such as what you used to call each other?
I always called my mother "Maman", and the other one "Laulau", because her name was Laurence. They separated quite early on, so I don't have many memories of them living together. A few shouts, maybe, but it wasn't hard to live with, because these conflicts were rare.

You mentioned your "mother". Don't you think Laulau is a mother in the truest sense of the word?

It depends on how you define mother. What's certain is that my biological mother will always be my mother. And the other is a parent: I can't deny that, that's the truth. But I don't know at what point you start talking about "mother". I know she's always been with me. So she's a mother on a psychological level, but I have no blood ties with her or her family. So it's different. It's not a rejection! Just an observation.

Does genetics really matter to you?
Yes, but I'm still young. Maybe I'll change my mind!

What do you know about the legal recognition or rights of Laurence, your social mother?
I know she's recognized by the courts as my legal guardian: she can accompany me, make requests, but there are things she can't do. For example, she had a problem with the hospital over insurance issues, because she's not related to me by blood.

So there are still some inequalities between your two parents?
Laulau has fewer rights over me than my biological mother.

How do you see it? Do you think this should change in your case?
It's justice, so I don't question it. I've never had a problem with it, even though I know there are special cases where it can pose a problem. If there's an inequality, it's not important. If I have to go to hospital, it's my mother who goes with me: what's the problem?

Have there ever been any conflicts between your two mothers, over custody, for example, or over any rights they might have over you?

12. Interview with Nathan, 16

Not about rights, no. There was never any dispute about any rights they had over us. They made children together: they're both parents in the same way. That's not the case with custody. When they split up, they wanted to have me with them. At first, they argued a bit about who would have which week, who would have the weekend, who would have Wednesday... Eventually, things settled down and there have been no problems since.

How important is your biological father to you?

When I was little, I was very attached to him, because all my friends talked about "father". Since I didn't have one, I had to be attached to something. The biological father is a kind of ideal father (I imagine him tall and handsome, of course!), but I have friends who have complicated fathers, who get beaten up by them. I've never experienced that. So, today, I'd like to meet him.

Do you have any information about your donor?

I know he's from the Liège region of Belgium. My parents told me he must be a doctor or medical student, because a lot of people who donate are doctors. Thanks to my looks, I can imagine what he looks like, but I don't have much information on that.

What do you think of the famous "father figure" in your own family situation?

The father is perhaps what's missing in my family. I know, for example, that he's Belgian, so we're a bit attached to Belgium. We go there sometimes. The father's origins are important. But, in everyday life, it's not a real lack, even if it's something I'd like to have.

Have you ever talked to your mothers about this desire to meet your father?
Often.

And?
Every time, it's the same story: impossible.

Do you think it's possible for a family to "do without" a father?
The proof is that I'm not dead yet! But the presence of a father can help, as he has a big part to play in a child's upbringing. My parents are members of an association called APGL, where they are in contact with many other homoparental couples. So I have a lot of friends who are in my situation, and I've noticed that when the family is different, for example when it's a single-parent family, there's always a lack of self-confidence, like a weakness. I have a friend who can't speak for himself: he listens to others and repeats what they say. I have another friend who expresses this by talking too much: he talks all the time and, as a result, you can see that he's not at ease.

Was the donor the same for you as for your brother?
Yes, we were very lucky to have the same one.

How important is this to you?
If we hadn't had the same donor, my brother wouldn't have been one hundred percent my brother. But then, my moms raised me with my brother: in any case, he would have been my brother, even if there might have been a doubt.

What representations of sexuality, sexual orientation and gender identity has your family situation created in you?

I don't think it makes any difference whether you come from a same-sex couple or not, at least in terms of your child's orientation. For example, I am and always have been straight, and so is my little brother, but I also have friends who grew up in homoparental families who are not. It's got nothing to do with the parents' orientation, even if, when that's the case, it's better accepted by homosexual couples!

Do you think you're aware of the discrimination faced by queer and LGBTQIA+ people?

Yes. Too much, in fact. I think we live in a society that's a bit too attentive to minorities. It's great that *gay* marriage is allowed, that everyone has the right to be whatever they want, but there's a kind of fashion effect when certain people claim to be I don't know what.

On the subject of these demands, do you feel concerned by the debates on marriage for all, PMA or GPA?

I'm not interested. I saw that my parents were following the story, but I'm not interested.

Have you ever wondered why?

It's simple: I'm not *gay*. If I have children, it will be with a woman.

Has your family experience led you to question what we might call femininity?

Not really, no. For me, a woman is a woman, a man is a man. I'm not a woman, so I can't judge; I don't know what it is and I respect it.

How do you feel about your family situation, your extended family, your friends and your school environment? Have your feelings on the subject changed since you were younger?

With friends, no worries. Nor with family. I've always been close to my family, whether on my biological mother's side or the other. I'm part of both their families. I think there's always been something different about my biological mother, but I know my little brother doesn't feel that way. He doesn't care about genetic origins or biology.

How were your mothers accepted into each other's families?

I've never felt that one of the mothers was in conflict with the other family. In general, it was very well accepted. That said, they split up relatively early in my life, so I don't remember much about it. But I do know that each retains contacts and friends in the other's family.

Have you sensed a shared sense of belonging, a community of identity between children from the same type of family configuration, within the PLGA you mentioned, for example?

In terms of family configuration, never. But I have a lot of friends who were conceived like us in Belgium. It's as if we had some kind of father in common. I'm much more attached to them. We have a way of belonging together. When I'm with them, it's like we're brothers and sisters.

13.
Maloë, age 14

My name is Maloë. Maloë Raso-Bouré to my family and friends. Maloë Raso to the State. That's the whole story, or almost. I'm 14 years old, and I live in Brittany. And I have two moms: Anne, a PE teacher at my current collège, and Émilie, a CPE at my future lycée.

My story begins in the 2000s. Two women, Anne and Émilie, fall in love. They fell in love, entered into a civil partnership and, after a few years, wanted to extend their family. So they resorted to PMA. They decided that Anne would carry their baby. After numerous appointments, tests and visits, they went to Belgium for insemination, i.e. the injection of donor sperm. Emilie and Anne chose an anonymous donor. After a fortnight, Anne took a pregnancy test. It was positive. The pregnancy went very well. On September 8, 2006, the two mothers-to-be went to hospital to prepare for delivery, but the baby wouldn't come out. In the end, I was born on September 16 by Caesarean section, induced during the night. My mothers were delighted.

Alas, two years later, Anne and Emilie, by mutual agreement, parted ways. I have no memory of the time they were together, so seeing them separated is a habit for me. They explained to me that, even if they don't love each other anymore, they'll always love me. When they split up, they each got their own apartment. So I've experienced the joys of alternating custody. From Monday to Wednesday mornings, I went to Mama Anne's. Wednesday afternoons and

Thursdays, I went to my mother's. Wednesday afternoons-Thursdays-Fridays, I went to Mommy Emilie's. For the *weekend,* I'd go to Anne's, and the following week, I'd spend it with Émilie, and so on... This meant I could see them regularly. From what my moms tell me, I wasn't any more disturbed than that by this alternating custody arrangement. My moms stayed on good terms, because I was their priority. To this day, the three of us have snacks together, and they often talk about me.

During my three years in kindergarten, all my friends and their parents knew that I had two moms and no dad, because I often talked about it. No one cared. When I arrived in the "big leagues", in first grade, Émilie fell in love with Gwenaël, known as Gwen. He was 13 years younger than her. When Maman Émilie asked me to meet him, I refused.

- Why?

- I don't feel like it.

Eventually I met him, and the three of us moved into a house. I had a lot of trouble with him, maybe because he was a man and I was used to living with women. For his part, Gwen also had trouble with me, as he was still young and not used to living with a 6-year-old girl who demanded attention. Nevertheless, I now had two moms, two places to live and a stepfather.

At school, when I said I had two moms, some of my girlfriends said:

- It's not possible, we have to have a dad.

One day, a girlfriend even said to me:

- Emilie, did she carry you in her belly?

- No.

- So she's not your mother!

- And your father?

- What, Father?

- Did he carry you in his belly?

- Well, no!

- So he's not your father.

My "girlfriend" wasn't entirely wrong, though: I didn't have a father. A father is someone who raises his child, whether he's the biological father or not. My biological father doesn't know me, he didn't raise me and he knows it. So, for me, he's my *sire*, the being who passed on his genes to me, nothing more. The incessant reflections and questions from my friends were starting to get on my nerves, because I didn't understand why they didn't understand and they didn't understand why I didn't understand that they didn't understand, etc. My lack of understanding was based on the fact that I didn't know what I was talking about. My lack of understanding could be summed up in six words: as far as I was concerned, my family was normal. Period.

On top of that, for a while, the "big kids", the CM2s, would follow me to every recess to ask me questions, and always the same ones. I ended up feeling totally different, and that saddened me. My memories are hazy, but I remember my moms talking to my teacher about it, and she must have talked to the CM2s about it, because after that day, I never got any more embarrassing questions from them.

In July 2014, I was finishing my CE2 when Gwen, my stepfather, and mom Émilie gave birth to Awen, a little boy. Even though I had no blood relationship with him since Gwen was my stepfather and Mommy Émilie was not my biological mother, I immediately considered him (and still do) as my little brother. As for Mama Anne, as far as I know, she had only a few one-night stands.

During the summer vacations, between CM2 and 6e, Mum Émilie and Mum Anne moved at the same time to another part of

13. Maloë, age 14

Brittany, where the college where Anne worked was located. So I left my friends behind. As I didn't want a repeat of what I'd experienced in first grade, I only told a few friends that I had two moms. That way, I escaped any disparaging remarks.

Today I'm in 3rd grade and I'm not going to shout *it* out in the middle of the playground. But if anyone asks, I never lie.

When people ask me if I'd like to meet my father, I say no, not particularly, and I don't care if it's impossible anyway. I live very well as I am, and I don't feel the need to have a father around. When I was little, I used to imagine him tall, with long blond hair and a tan. I also thought he must be a generous man, because he helps a lot of families by donating his sperm. I like to imagine that if the donor has made other sperm donations, I've probably got lots of "half-siblings" out there in the world!

For the moment, I consider myself straight, but if one day I fall in love with a girl, I know my moms will be happy for me. Homosexuals are just like straight people. It's only their sexual orientation that's different. That's up to them.

In today's society, gay rights and acceptance are not progressing far enough. Here's an example. My moms and I applied to have me carry both their surnames. I was refused. So, as far as the French state is concerned, my name is Maloë Raso. In reality, I'm Maloë Raso-Bouré, and I'm happy and proud to have two mothers who love me.

14.
Interview with Arya and Ariel, age 13

Could you briefly introduce yourself?

ARYA: My name is Arya, and I'm 13 years old. I have two moms, and I'm here to talk about my family, which is normal.

ARIEL : My name is Ariel, I'm 13 years old. I have two mothers and a twin sister.

What do you know about your design?

ARIEL: My mothers went to Holland so that when we turned sixteen, we could find out who our donor was. We were conceived by PMA.

Were you adopted by your "social" mother?

ARYA: The mother who gave birth to us is legally our mother. Through marriage in 2013, our other mother adopted us, and they are both our parents.

Where do you live?

ARYA: In the Drôme.

ARIEL: In Montélimar.

Do you talk to your classmates about your family situation?

ARYA: Yes, and I didn't notice any reactions. We moved around a lot, and when we went to a new school, I'd tell the friends I made straight away if anyone asked. I got a few nasty remarks, but on the whole it was fine.

Ariel: Up until primary school, I didn't have any problems. It was towards the beginning of middle school that I said *it* a lot less. I find that in fifth and fourth grade, people are more open. When you arrive and tell them you have two mothers, you don't have to explain why or how.

Have you ever been asked about concrete aspects of homoparenting?

Ariel: It was mostly in primary school that we were asked. We always explained. Often, we'd bring books that explained the subject so that the teachers could explain it in turn. In middle school, you don't need to explain too much. Most people know what it means.

Arya: I don't dwell on the subject. My friends know. Some people go, "Oh, you've got two moms?" and then they say, "Well, how can that be?" Then they say, "But how can that be?" and all that... In that case, I don't answer them, I just say, "There, I've got two moms", period. Otherwise, things can get out of hand. I remember once, in seventh grade, someone asked me if I was a lesbian.

And what were the reactions in your family, particularly from your grandparents?

Ariel: Moderately until we were born. Before that, they weren't very hot.

Arya: Afterwards, they were normal grandparents: we love them, they love us...

What about the other members of your family?

Arya: Our cousins are about the same age as us...

Ariel: We know them, and they're very nice to us, so everything's fine.

Do you perceive a difference between acceptance in your "social" mother's family and in your "biological" mother's family?
Arya: Maybe it was easier on our "social" mother's side, but... No, actually, no, I don't think so.

I've used the terms "biological mother" and "social mother". What do you call them?
Ariel: We say "our mothers".
Arya: "Our parents."
Ariel: We gave them different names: "Maman" and "Ména".

Do you know any other rainbow families? Have you been involved with the APGL?
Arya: Our parents are members of the APGL. So we have friends who also have same-sex families.
Ariel: We see them about twice a year.

Are your mothers involved in defending the rights of same-sex families?
Arya: Of course! We go to Gay Prides, we demonstrate... Our parents are part of the Drôme APGL committee. They're politically committed.
Ariel: Our moms had a front-row seat during the debates on "marriage for all", as one of them was spokesperson for the APGL at the time.

14. Interview with Arya and Ariel, age 13

How do you see the future of rainbow children?

Arya: Very, very good! I can see the improvements. For example, there are now kids in middle school who realize they're gay. They say it like that, and I'm very happy that it's so open.

Did growing up in a rainbow family make you more open about gender identity or sexual orientation?

Ariel: It makes you think. At first, you say you're different from the others and you wonder why, and then you think: what difference does it make?

Anything to add?

Arya: Live as you please!

15.
Anouk, 18 years old

My biological mother underwent artificial insemination in the Netherlands with sperm purchased in the United States. She and her partner wanted to choose the donor, which is not possible in European countries. Originally, my second mother was supposed to carry us, but it didn't work out.

From my "donor" I know that he was a Taiwanese immigrant to Arizona, that he was a bodybuilder, and that his sister was a model and that he had no vision problems. These were things that were in his file and that my moms - especially my "social mom" who always denied me access to the file - told us. Anyway, I don't need to know any more. I don't have and I don't want a relationship with this person. For me, a donor is just sperm. From the start, it was clear that I had two mothers, period.

Of course, I don't introduce myself by saying: "Hello, my name is Anouk, I have two mothers". But if I have to talk about the parents' professions, I always say: "Mother's profession" and re-"Mother's profession". I never hide who I am, because I have nothing to hide. My biological mother always took care of the forms a bit more, but I always had both of them sign the papers, even if one of them wasn't legally entitled to.

Their status is a little different: my biological mother is officially my mother and, for the past few months, my social mother has officially adopted me and my sister as simple adoptees - although, in my eyes, that doesn't change anything. My parents are my mothers. For me, the term "parents" doesn't mean a father and a mother. It just means: the people who raised a child, with whom you spent a lot of time. In a pinch, it could even mean an animal! In Truffaut's *L'Enfant sauvage,* the child was raised by wolves, so his parents would be wolves.

Yet adoption remains a complicated process. It requires testimonials, memories, photos, letters... Of course, the aim is to protect against abuse. But the result is that it's even more complicated when it involves two homosexuals; and, in the end, such a process requires a sacrifice because, when I was adopted, my biological mother lost her parental authority so that my social mother could obtain it.

For my part, I was lucky enough to be educated in privileged schools where the other students were open and tolerant. Despite this, I remember being bothered by the recurrent idea that a couple implies a father and a mother. In an SVT book, there was a quick passage on PMA, specifying that it was reserved for heterosexual couples... and that was probably fine. Nor was there any mention of the ecological dimension of the birth rate. Why continue to procreate? If you want to have a child, all you have to do is adopt, so as not to increase the demographic pressure on the planet's reserves. Since adoption is complicated, let's push to simplify the process!

In the meantime, it's time to rebuild our own standards, both internal and external. For example, even though I have two mothers, I've always seen heterosexuality as the norm. When I met other children living with same-sex couples, I was amazed to meet people like us. We seemed to share an exceptional characteristic! This made me realize that I had internalized the social functioning that distinguishes the heterosexual norm from the homosexual exception.

Not enough to convince me that I belong to the vast LGBTQIA+ community. I'm sensitive to the fights for equal rights waged by the *queer* movement; I go to specialized festivals because I appreciate the young filmmakers I discover there; I hung a rainbow flag in my student room because, born into a homoparental family, I didn't choose to immerse myself in this issue any more than a homosexual chooses to construct himself as *gay*. It has to be said that I've got a lot on my plate! I'm also Eurasian in appearance, even though I'm Taiwanese only in my donor gametes; and I have a dual Franco-Germanic culture thanks to my two mothers. It's quite paradoxical because, in my head, I'm 100% Franco-French. It's only in the gaze of others or the reflection in my mirror that I'm thrown back on questions of intersectionality...

My racialization allows me to get to grips with the idea of "weird". Most of my family is white, and I look Asian... But when I talk to Asian people, I feel like I'm behaving like a white person because I have white ideas. So I *see* my interlocutor's difference as others see my difference. Conversely, when I talk to a German, I feel as if I share the same codes, even though I have nothing Germanic in my blood.

The downside of my Eurasian appearance is the racism it entails. I remember that, in February 2020, when the Wuhan coronavirus was starting to seriously shake things up, I coughed as I sat on the metro. The passenger in front of me looked up. When he saw a Chinese woman coughing, he got up in a hurry and left the car at the next station! At the time, having abused the weed, let's just say my mind was a little foggy, so I thought the incident was funny. It was only afterwards that I thought about amalgams, their sometimes ridiculous, sometimes hurtful, sometimes dangerous side. The *ni hao* or *ching chang chong* that people throw at me in the street when I come home at night.

So, just as I'm concerned about *gay* rights, I'm concerned about racism. I've recently come to terms with my slant eyes, my skin color and my appearance. I used to blame my mothers for taking an Asian donor when they had the choice of taking someone white, for example. Now I appreciate being the racialized child of two lesbians, which is why I wrote the following.

*

FIVE TIPS FOR SURVIVING IN SOCIETY WHEN YOU HAVE TWO MOTHERS

A child or adult who reveals that he or she has been raised by two mothers is likely to be confronted very quickly with the inescapable stupidity of human beings. He or she will be asked questions that no one would ask a child with one father and one mother. The subject can quickly become embarrassing. That's why it's important to appear less outraged than detached or even amused. Keeping your sense of humor and repartee is essential - developing it can be vital. Especially as the longer this kind of conversation goes on, the less bearable it becomes. Here's my advice.

1. Anticipate your response options on classics that accompany the Revelation of your status as a "child of a lesbian," such as:
- Oh, uh, ah, uh, uh, ah yeah anyway.
- Are your mothers lesbians? You don't look like it!
- You don't? Well, don't worry, it's not a big deal, it doesn't change anything between us, I'm very open-minded.

- So how does it work?

- So, they're allowed to adopt, the, uh, homos? I didn't know...

- How is it possible to have two moms? There's a real one, isn't there?

- How often do you see your father? What does he think?

- OK, so I guess you don't have much choice, are you *gay* too?

2. Once you've practiced your answers, move on to phase 2 of the exercise: **invent** other stupid reactions. It's a pretty amazing exercise. Make the most of it - it's one of the rare occasions when you're allowed to be homophobic and remain politically correct.

Stand in front of a mirror, ideally on the same level. Inhale through your mouth, exhale through your nose and alternate between the two roles. Study your reactions. This exercise can be filmed for review and analysis. Don't forget to congratulate yourself if you've achieved your objectives.

3. During your school years, especially in junior high and high school, **have fun** with teachers by sending your parents alternately to parent-teacher meetings. If you do it right and come up with a clever, well-thought-out plan, you can drive the teachers crazy without suffering any consequences. They'll be ashamed of having had homophobic thoughts.

This is true of many of the situations we encourage you to create yourself. You'll get some good laughs out of them, and remember them at painful family reunions - family reunions, that is.

4. Renounce the assumption of violence, even in the face of ill-intentioned people. That's right, even with big jerks. Words are often stronger. They highlight your intellectual superiority, your general culture and your wit.

15. Anouk, 18 years old

Of course, a pie in the face or a punch in the face are often tempting. Resist, prove that you exist: a good joke or a good speech is more effective than a clumsy jab, or one barely toned enough to swat fly droppings.

5. Prepare a small reservoir of *punchlines*. Truth be told, few are specific to kids lucky enough to have two moms; but there's one that kids with two dads won't steal from us. Classic, even *vintage*.

- Zyva, fuck your mother!

we can always answer:

- Which one?

Having two mothers isn't always easy? Come on, that's no reason to feel sorry for yourself! Dare to navigate the ocean of homophobic silliness with finesse, and your two moms will be an excellent asset to your social life.

Conclusion

Everyone who testifies here tells us they have something to say. That they have their voice.

That no one will speak for them.

They show us that children from lesboparental backgrounds are, as such, nothing extraordinary. This apparent normality also means that our families are not entirely free of gender norms and stereotypes. The lives sketched out here follow conventional paths, which can be traced back to their social background and sociological profile, and not to the sexual orientation of their mothers. This notwithstanding, rainbow children undoubtedly benefit from privileged access to political or associative commitment to the recognition of *queer* and LGBTQIA+ people in general, insofar as their sensitivity to this subject is heightened by their family situation.

Many of our witnesses live in blended families. For children conceived by MAP, as for children from previous heteroparental constellations, step-parents and new "adelphs", as we call siblings, are fully recognized.

It's worth noting that the much-debated issue of access to origins is not an obsession for the witnesses: "origins" generally fuel curiosity, and sometimes desire. None of the children expressed deep frustration on this subject. However, the distinction between biological and social mothers, which is often made, creates a new binarity, as if being a "biological mother" conferred a privileged place on only one of the people who also desired, who also loved, who also fought to be able to give birth to the children with whom the state prevents them from living fully. Rainbow children all place love and desire at the heart of their family and identity construction. These poles do not replace the aspiration for full legal recognition: the refusal by the state apparatus to grant parental authority to one of the mothers and the lack of legal recognition of filiation are clearly identified as the main obstacles to the full development of rainbow children.

Many witnesses have been adopted by their social mother. This was also my case. I'm happy to finally have two official mothers, and I can measure the happiness of those who have seen this concrete filiation finally recognized by the State. Some mothers choose to marry in order to achieve this. In other cases, social mothers adopt their children when they come of age. Such recognition is the least we can do, not a privilege. Our families are recognized as such only after a huge delay compared with heteroparental families, for whom no question arises.

This invites us to open up the paradigms of filiation and kinship. What Michel Foucault said in 1981 takes on a crucial meaning today: according to him,

> if we ask people to reproduce the marriage bond so that their personal relationship is recognized, the progress made is slight. We live in a relational world that institutions have considerably impoverished. Society and the institutions that form its backbone have limited the possibility of relationships, because a rich relational world would be extremely complicated to manage. We have to fight against this impoverishment of the relational fabric.[12]

---

12. Michel Foucault, "Le triomphe social du plaisir sexuel: une conversation avec Michel Foucault" (interview with G. Barbedette, October 20, 1981), *in: Dits et écrits,*

The aim is to considerably expand relational possibilities and, while fighting for formal rights and recognition by the state, to think up new modes of filiation.

Some contributors have expressed discomfort with the idea of testifying, in the sense that their testimony could be perceived as justification, as a way of apologizing for growing up in rainbow families. By containing embodied accounts of lived experience, this collection aims precisely to help ensure that we no longer have to justify ourselves for being who we are.

Taken as a whole, these testimonials prove that growing up in a lesboparental environment doesn't hinder an individual's formation or autonomy. It doesn't hinder thinking, emancipation or self-fulfilment. The sixteen stories also point out that such situations are not inherently preferable to others. In other words, there's nothing exceptional about being a rainbow child. The only advantage: being able to talk about it with full knowledge of the facts.

If the stories collected here serve as a reminder that tenderness, love, affection and desire are more than enough to structure family configurations and legitimize new modes of filiation, then this collection will have fulfilled its role. In fact, the first step towards recognition is to understand the multiplicity of family situations, the diversity of ways of desiring together and building a shared existence, and therefore to listen to what the people concerned have to say about themselves.

These testimonies, simple samples of the astonishing diversity of filial possibilities to which it is necessary to facilitate access, are not intended to allow rainbow children to apologize for not having a father in the traditional sense of the term, nor to emphasize

---

1954-1988, tome IV, Paris, Gallimard, 1994, pp. 309-310.

that one is not responsible for one's family configuration. On the contrary, it's about freeing ourselves from the grip of what we call "cisheteronormativity" and, in so doing, proving that it's possible to think and desire outside Western heteropatriarchal norms.

Although PMA is now available to more people in France, let's not rest on this achievement or imagine that the process of emancipation is complete. On the contrary, it's only just begun.

Gender binarity remains an essential structure of our society. Even today, modes of domination linked to gender and sexual orientation, class and racial oppression, validism, ageism and infantilization are fundamental components of our heterocapitalist society. The dominant power won't grant anything by itself: struggles and fights are more necessary than ever to wrest real rights and gain full recognition.

Let's be part of this movement.

Let's fight for equality.

Afterword.
Kolia, 21 years old

Two mothers gave birth to me in the summer of 1999, 21 years before I coordinated this book.

Two mothers.

If I sometimes speak of my "social" mother and my "biological" mother, it's only by convention and for the sake of clarity: otherwise, the biological is not a relevant criterion for distinguishing my two mothers. In fact, I speak more often of "my German mother" and "my French mother". Not that nationality is a more appropriate criterion, but growing up in a Franco-German context has the advantage of not having to present my mothers in biological terms. A daily battle. When I was a little younger, my school friends would often ask me: "But who's your real mother, then? It's always been clear to me that my mothers are both my *social* mothers, in the sense that the family itself is a social institution: they're equal.

Equal - but not in the eyes of the law. My social mother was eventually able to adopt my sister and me, so that she could be recognized as our mother. Nevertheless, for twenty years, I only had one mother in administrative terms. Yet I've always asserted their equality. They've always been my mothers in the same way: I love them, they love me and they've been a significant part of my life.

In fact, I've never used the term "mom" to address one of my mothers, as I would have had to find another term to address the other and, in so doing, discriminate against them. However, I know that many rainbow children use this lexicon.

*

It's strange that a person with slanting eyes should be born on this day, when neither of his mothers can claim Asian ancestry. This physical trait comes from my "donor" (whom I prefer to call "my donor-x"[13]), who was living in the United States at the time, and whose family is of Hong Kong-Taiwanese origin. These eyes, perceived as slanted, which I share with my sister, three years my junior, are a decisive element in the construction of my identity. Ordinary racism structures my existence to the same degree as the lesbophobia suffered by a rainbow child in an indirect way, and the fact that I am racialized is all the more important as most of the contributors to this collection are not.

Up to now, I've been accumulating two oppressions: not only the indirect one linked to my mothers' sexual and romantic orientation, but also the oppression of race.

Things are more complicated when it comes to class. I come from what you might call the intellectual petit bourgeoisie. One of my mothers is developing a "more responsible" digital lifestyle, while the other characterizes herself as a *"serial drifter in the arts & words domain".* They share a commitment to the environment. One

---

131. It may come as a surprise that I've chosen to write this term in inclusive language. After all, don't we speak of "a donor"? I've decided to stop talking about "my donor", breaking with a family habit, insofar as, not knowing this person, the only "masculine" elements we can attribute to him are his primary sexual characteristics and his hormonal system. However, it seems disrespectful to me to perpetuate this mythology by gendering this person masculine when I know no more about his gender identity than I do about how he wishes to be gendered: who knows, perhaps this person is non-binary or trans?

started out as a high-school economics teacher, while the other was an actress, until they met, decided to make music together, ended up separating some fifteen years ago, and my sister and I grew up with them in alternating custody, in the eighteenth and tenth arrondissements of Paris.

*

If, in referring to my birth, I spoke of myself as a "being", in a neutral way, it's because I was assigned the male gender at birth, whereas today I identify myself as a transgender person.

When the idea for this collection of testimonials was born, at the end of 2019, I hadn't yet made my trans *coming-out*; the progression of my transition has, in temporal terms, coincided with the construction of this book. In fact, these two initiatives are linked. Both express a desire for *affirmation*. My transition expresses my need to assert my gender identity, while the creation of this collection of testimonies from rainbow children stems from a desire to highlight the uniqueness of our *rainbow families*.

These two assertions are profoundly political, insofar as they concern the equality of people's public visibility, the question of which bodies can move around without fear of being attacked because of their identity, who can talk about themselves and their history without shame, which people have which rights, and which bodies are considered political subjects in their own right.

I can already hear the opponents of *rainbow families* claiming that it was inevitable that a family based on two mothers, and therefore on an alleged lack of a father, would produce disturbed, disoriented, unstructured children. This would presuppose that transidentity would express such a disturbance, and would mean

Afterword. Kolia, 21 years old

that the romantic or sexual orientation of the parents would determine or, *at the very least,* have an effect on that of the children. I reject both the first statement and the second, and I'm relying on the hypothesis - because it's only a possibility - that living in a *queer* or LGBTQIA+ environment could have the advantage of showing children that reproducing heteronormative arrangements is only one way of living, and that there are an infinite number of others, even if they are, for the time being, in the minority.

In saying this, I'm in no way suggesting that children living in heteroparental settings would be less open-minded than we are. That would be a contemptuous and unequal position! I'm simply saying that the majority heteroparental structure doesn't facilitate access to other family possibilities, since it meets the normative criteria of the experienced structure.

*

To those who argue against multicolored parentage, I also reply that, like many rainbow children, I followed a classic academic path: lettres sup', Normale Sup' - I think there's enough "sup" in such a *curriculum* to satisfy those who still believe that rainbow children would necessarily lead an existence outside the paths valued by our society. Still, I shouldn't even have to show my credentials: does a person have to have followed this kind of path to be fully recognized? Even if I had followed an alternative, socially devalued path, I would still be affirming my status as a rainbow child aspiring to full social and intersubjective recognition.

By speaking of intersubjective recognition, I'm suggesting that institutional and social recognition is only part of the recognition I aspire to. "Intersubjective", because it's often in reactions and

micro-reactions that the most common LGBTQIA+phobia mani-
fests itself. I've lost count of the number of times I've uttered the
fateful "I have two mothers", regretting it immediately afterwards,
perceiving the effect of disgust or more or less disguised disap-
proval that such a statement can cause.

But I also want to say that it's frequently the intersubjective relationship that provokes my inhibition and fear.

To say it.

That I have two mothers.

Today, I assert this family background with a vengeance - this
collection is proof of that. However, it took me some time to free
myself from this feeling of shame. It made me cautious. It made me

to avoid answering directly when my classmates in the sixth form
asked me who the person was who picked me up at the school gate;

to remain discreet during the debates surrounding "marriage for
all" and to leave the floor to those who are not concerned;

to be terrified of handing in the back-to-school form on which
I was supposed to indicate "father's profession";

to hide so as not to have to face the teacher's gaze which would
unmask me;

to lie by omission;

to keep things ambiguous;

to do everything to delay the moment of clarification, to post-
pone the scene of truth.

Over time, I became stronger.

Thanks partly to the kindness and profoundly *safe* nature of the
people I befriended in high school, and partly to my growing politicization, I was able to convert this sense of shame into strength, into
a desire to fight that was closely linked to a political approach to the
social world: my struggle for full recognition of family arrangements

similar to mine was increasingly linked to a desire to change the world, to overturn the "present state of things", to use Marx and Engels' formula in *The German Ideology*. The current state of affairs is the negation of equality. Our fight for recognition as rainbow children is part of a general dynamic of emancipation.

That's why I've always opposed rhetoric that reduces institutional recognition of rainbow families to a societal measure far removed from the social struggles and progressive aspirations of the radical left.

The most problematic was the *denial of* the lesboparental dimension of my family when I was told:

- Come on, Kolia, you have a father!

Seemingly infallible logic: everyone has a father, whether they know him or not. So they knew my truth for me. As if a family without a father were inconceivable. I'm not saying I don't have a "donor", I'm saying I don't have a father. A crucial distinction: the person who donated is not part of my family. I don't know them, and I have no desire to get to know them. In other words, I have no desire for contact with the origin.

Nevertheless, this indifference to my "origins" is not political indifference, since the fact that I am racialized leads me to feel concerned by questions of coloniality and postcoloniality. I would say that my racialization allows me not to dissociate politics and the world, given that, although I'm of French nationality, I feel foreign here, in France, by virtue of a quite significant postcolonial parameter that structures imperialist Europe. So I think it's worth mentioning that when I'm asked "Where are you from?", I can interpret this question in terms of both my racialization and my parentage. I come from nowhere, if you need a father to come from somewhere, to have an "origin" and not to be structured by a "lack"; I'm perceived as non-European by most people living on the European continent - so that, wherever I may be, I may be asked if I speak French, and then, once I've proved that I have some command of the language, what my "origins" are.

*

I'd like to delve deeper into the question of my racialization.

I know that this term offends a certain number of people, insofar as it is based on the term "race", and the use of the latter is often misunderstood. If, as is customary in anti-racist and decolonial activism and theorizing, I speak of "racization", it is in a social and political sense that has nothing to do with a racist position. On the contrary, it is precisely against the various forms of racism that it is used. Indeed, the term racisation denotes the social process by which certain bodies are minorized, excluded, marginalized or exploited.

It's difficult for me to identify with the experience of a white rainbow child, *id est* non-racialized, because the parameter of racialization is, in my experience, highly significant.

Firstly, because when I'm seen with my mothers, I'm generally perceived as an adoptee, which isn't the case since I was conceived by MAP.

Secondly, and this point is linked to the previous one, because I'm perceived as a foreigner who doesn't speak French. A non-racialized rainbow child is never confronted with this kind of racism towards people perceived as Asian or Eurasian.

Finally, I've often wondered about the implications of being a racialized person with two non-racialized mothers: as white people, they don't have my experiences any more than I have theirs.

There are few racialized people in my extended family. I feel like a stranger in my own home (and this is not limited to the family, but structures my daily life). I have no images of racialized people, no stories of racialized people, few racialized people in my circle...

I'll be told that my experience corresponds to that of any racialized person, and that this experience is independent of my identity as a rainbow child. If I hadn't been conceived by artificial insemination and born in France, the probability of my not being racialized would have been much greater.

*

This brings me to what I call my libidinal orientation (an adjective that refers to desire and denotes the sexual as well as the romantic). The greatest fear - and at the same time the greatest certainty - of opponents of rainbow families is fueled by the idea that the children of LGBTQIA+ people are determined to mimic the sexual and romantic orientation of their parents. I identify as a lesbian myself, which seems to support this position. In reality, it's not impossible that growing up with two mothers and no father(s) made me aware of a non-masculine presence. What's next? Do we question heterosexual people born of heterosexual parents in the same way?

There's no need to point out that our society is heteronormative: heterosexuality and heteromanticism are fully accepted and perceived as neutral, whereas alternative forms of sexual or romantic orientation are still perceived as deviant and socially repressed, if not entirely ignored or denied (I'm thinking of the treatment or non-treatment reserved for bisexuals, pansexuals, panromantics, asexuals, aromantics...). One of the reasons for this non-acceptance is profound: any romantic or sexual relationship that doesn't conform to the schema of reproduction or, *ipso facto,* to gender binarity, is socially devalued. But if I'm generally attracted to people who don't identify with cismasculinity, that doesn't mean I exclude all other types of desire, without identifying myself as pansexual or panromantic.

When I speak of heteronormative arrangements, I'm not implying that my family is outside any norm, that it doesn't reproduce any standard pattern. Acceptance of my transition was not easy for my mothers, which simply shows that, as in any family, filial relationships are not the most conducive to openness. I'd even go further and say that it's the family structure as such that makes full acceptance of bodies impossible, insofar as the modern Western family implies a dependency between its members that causes them to want to impose their will on others, particularly within the power relationships between parents and children.

The reason I say this is to consider the family in itself, and not to pretend that rainbow families are free of any power relationships or inequalities. I have no intention of lecturing conventional family configurations!

*

I came out of the closet at a time when work on this collection was already well advanced. It is therefore linked, on the one hand, to the desire to affirm modes of existence that are not accepted by Western heterocapitalist society and, on the other, to my desire to fight against lesbophobia, transphobia and, more broadly, the oppression suffered by *queer* and LGBTQIA+ people.

I'm not the only one who's tired of suffering the non-acceptance and lack of recognition of the equality of all bodies. Many of us can no longer bear to settle for the crumbs thrown our way by the state. We can never ask for enough. We need to move away from debate, discussion and compromise, in order to devote all our energy to the fight for equality and to defeating all positions hostile to collective emancipation and the self-determination of bodies and individuals. Such positions are intolerable because they are profoundly false. So any struggle against the unequal order - and against the reactionary right, which justifies this order - is right, insofar as it takes the side of truth.

We affirm and prove this truth, the truth of our experience as minoritized bodies, with this collection of testimonies from rainbow children; all you have to do is check it out.

Table of contents

The *making of*..7

Foreword by Martine Gross, sociologist 11

1. Anne-Lise, 25 years old 15

2. Interview with Audrey, 26 25

3. Sasha, 22 years old...33

4. Interview with Elsa, 20 41

5. Alex, aged 22 47

6. Interview with Aurore, 20 57

7. Léa, 23 years old...63

Interlude The story of Mathilde, 23 71

8. Interview with Jeanne, 18, and Martin, 11 115

9. Laura, aged 31 123

10. Interview with Zoé, 18 131

11. Louise, 22 years old 135

12. Interview with Nathan, 16..141

13. Maloë, age 14..151

14. Interview with Arya and Ariel, age 13 155

15. Anouk, 18 years old 159

Conclusion 165

Afterword. Kolia, 21 years old...169

Best sellers Max Milo Editions

Hitler's banker, Jean-François Bouchard

Confessions of a forger, Éric Piedoie Le Tiec

The Koran and the flesh, Ludovic-Mohamed Zahed

Governing by fake news, Jacques Baud

Governing by chaos, Collectif

A political history of food, Paul Ariès

Mad in U.S.A.: The ravages of the "American model",
Michel Desmurget

Mondial soccer club geopolitics, Kévin Veyssière

Putin: Game master?, Jacques Braud

Treatise on the three impostors: Moses, Jesus, Muhammad,
The Spirit of Spinoza

TV Lobotomy, Michel Desmurget